Sherlock Holmes

MARK CAMPBELL

POCKET ESSENTIALS

This edition published in 2012 by Pocket Essentials
P.O.Box 394, Harpenden, Herts, AL5 1XJ
www.pocketessentials.com
Series Editor; Nick Rennison
Proofing and Index: Richard Howard

ISBN 978-1-84243-887-9

2 4 6 8 10 9 7 5 3

for Reg Gadney and Peter Haining, both guiding lights

Acknowledgements

For providing much needed information I am indebted to Richard Lancelyn Green, Roger Johnson, Roy Tunley, Peter Basham, Andy Lane, Paul Duncan, Iain Jarvis, Annick Barbery, Jean Barnham, Brett Nicholson, Craig Bowlsby and the friendly staff of the Slade Library, Plumstead. Thanks especially to the first three named, together with Jason Tomes, John Smart, my mum and my wife Mary, who proofread the manuscript and pointed out all my mistakes. And of course I mustn't forget Jesus, because he never forgets me.

Contents

CONTENTS

Foreword
by Richard Lancelyn Green

The fame of Sherlock Holmes goes beyond the known universe into the galaxies beyond, for the battered tin dispatch box which Watson left in the vaults of his bank and from which from time to time he extracted notes has produced a welter of new cases which show the Great Detective to be equally at home in the past, the present and the future. It is, however, the original cases which Dr Watson chronicled on which his fame rests and to which all readers should first turn. The 'canon' appeals on many levels. It is read by young and old and is uniquely the subject of 'higher criticism' which approaches the texts with all the care (if not the seriousness) which was once bestowed upon sacred books and classical authors. There are journals and societies devoted to Holmes, there are parodies and pastiches, and there have been numerous plays, films and other adaptations. It is a vast field, and yet Holmes remains a citizen of the world and is accessible to all.

This elegantly concise volume will serve as an excellent introduction and may be regarded as the modern equivalent of the old Baedeker Guide. If it leaves the reader anxious to visit Baker Street for the first time, or to revisit it for the umpteenth time, it will have served its purpose. It provides details of Holmes' creator and offers a critique of the Sherlock Holmes stories; it provides a sampler of the innumerable parodies and pastiches which they have inspired, and it breaks new ground by listing in alphabetical order the large number of actors who have played Sherlock Holmes, with the minor actors alongside the major ones, and the earliest with the latest.

Sherlock Holmes had with him a 'pocket Petrarch' in *The Boscombe Valley Mystery*, and he would be flattered to know that he was being honoured in the same way.

Richard Lancelyn Green
March 2001

Richard Lancelyn Green was a former chairman of the Sherlock Holmes Society of London and one of the foremost world experts on Conan Doyle and Sherlock Holmes. He edited the 1901 burlesque of William Gillette's play, Sheerluck Jones*, Penguin's* The Further Adventures of Sherlock Holmes, The Uncollected Sherlock Holmes *and* Letters to Sherlock Holmes, *and the Oxford World Classics Sherlock Holmes titles. With John Michael Gibson he wrote* A Bibliography of Arthur Conan Doyle. *Following his death in 2004, his extensive collection of Sherlockiana was bequeathed to the City of Portsmouth, where a permanent display was opened in June 2007.*

Please Continue Your Most Interesting Statement

It's difficult to imagine a world without Sherlock Holmes. But what if Arthur Conan Doyle had had a busier medical practice? Would he have had the time to write? And if he had, and his first major success had come with *Micah Clarke*, would he have even thought to create Holmes? Doyle was never as enamoured of the detective as he was of his historical stories, and it's unlikely the Baker Street sleuth would exist were it not for the doldrums he experienced at his Southsea practice.

Alternatively, what if Doyle was ill and never went to dinner with the editor of *Lippincott's Magazine*? *The Sign of Four* might never have been written and *Micah Clarke* would stand alone as a mildly interesting example of nineteenth century sensationalistic prose, a footnote in academic textbooks. And if neither of these two novels had been published, what would Doyle have written for *The Strand*? Brigadier Gerard a few years before his time? Professor Challenger two decades early? Perhaps we would have got Sherlock Holmes, perhaps not.

But this book is about what we *have* got. Four novels. Fifty-six short stories. The so-called 'sacred texts'. The Penguin editions sit next to me as I write this, in a little pile 11cm high, and I think Doyle would laugh if he knew the reverence people show to them. He was as good as he could be, but he was, when all is said and done, just a jobbing writer. A highly professional writer, but a jobbing one nonetheless. His Holmes was an entertainment, a diversion, a character he devoted just enough time to, and no more. His real interests lay elsewhere. He loved his romanticised historical fiction, exemplified by *Rodney Stone*. He loved his wives. He loved his country. He cared passionately about social justice and parity between the sexes. He championed the underdog. He believed in fairies.

If Doyle was still alive and you happened to mention Sherlock Holmes to him, I imagine that he would raise his eyebrows and say, 'Oh yes, *him*. Now, let's talk about something interesting.' Which should make us all the more grateful that we have such a rich legacy to look back on. The stories are (for the most part) beautifully crafted little tales, full of character, incident and revelation. Holmes is not an identikit set of characteristics, as has sometimes been claimed, and Watson is far from boring. Quite simply, they are real people caught up in real dramas. What is more, the bond of friendship between them is utterly believable, utterly *right*. Holmes needs Watson as much as Watson needs Holmes. They are mutually dependent – as all real friendships should be. One tense, intellectual, artistic; the other quiet, stable, sensible. They are like a comfortably married couple – only without the sex. Yes, even though they strolled along arm in arm once, please note their relationship is purely *platonic*; don't let anyone tell you otherwise.

There have been many attempts to fathom why these stories are so popular. Reading them again in one fell swoop for this guide I was struck by the number of similar themes:

- Holmes and Watson are rarely in danger (neither is ever imprisoned, tied up, kidnapped etc.).
- The good guys are obvious from the start (except, oddly

enough, in the four novels).
- Holmes invariably says, 'I have never seen such a singular case,' or words to that effect.
- The gender of letter writers is always obvious.
- Most of the crimes boil down to relationship problems (usually involving a *ménage à trois*).
- The murders are often hastily covered-up accidents or the result of *crime passionel*.
- The obvious culprit is always innocent.
- Holmes invariably takes the law into his own hands.
- The criminal, once discovered, normally says, in effect, 'It's a fair cop', and explains all.

These elements are part of a formula that makes the Sherlock Holmes stories so engaging. Familiarity breeds contempt, but it can also equally engender affection. Who but a robot does not feel a warm glow as Holmes stares out of the window at the glowering clouds, Watson glances through a medical journal, and the soft footfall of their next client is heard upon the stair? Who does not feel a strange thrill as the aforesaid client describes the mystery and Holmes interrupts to ask one of his peculiar questions? Ah, you think, he's onto it already. You sit back and let the story unfold around you, safe in the knowledge that the Great Detective is never wrong. (Well, hardly ever.)

Odd, then, that so much controversy rages over such gently absorbing stories. Sherlock Holmes aficionados have been debating for decades the dating of the stories, the precise location of 221B Baker Street, the number of Watson's marriages, the Christian names of the (three?) Moriartys, the cause of Holmes' misogyny, the disappearance of Watson's dog... the list of niggling inconsistencies goes ever on. Papers have been written, books published, speeches made. And we're still no closer to the truth. Which is, as I've said, that Doyle was a jobbing writer and the internal continuity of stories written over a period of forty years just did not interest him. And why should it?

If you visit Baker Street, you'll find a block of luxury apartments now straddling the famous 221B address, where the former Abbey National building once stood (it covered 215–229). But just down the street is the Sherlock Holmes Museum at the fictional 221B (actually 239). There you can curl up in front of a roaring fire with a deerstalker perched on your head while a young and attractive Mrs Hudson snaps your picture. And opposite you'll find a bright, friendly shop selling Sherlock Holmes memorabilia. You can witness at first hand the genuine props from the Granada TV series, guided by a chap in a grey ulster and deerstalker. It's all so damned... *British*. So whether you're new to the whole business, whether you've only seen a few Basil Rathbone films (and there's nothing wrong with that) or whether you're one of those who play 'The Great Game' and think Sherlock Holmes is real, I hope this short book provides a decent introduction to this quintessentially British phenomenon.

Sixty stories, millions of readers, three centuries of enjoyment.

Cheers, Sir Arthur. Thank goodness you weren't very busy.

Sir Arthur Conan Doyle

Arthur Conan Doyle ('Conan' derived from his great-uncle Michael Conan, a distinguished journalist) was born on 22 May 1859 at 11 Picardy Place, Edinburgh, the son of Charles Altamont Doyle and Mary (née Foley) and the second of ten children, of whom seven survived. Doyle's father was a civil servant and artist, and his grandfather John Doyle was known as the caricaturist 'HB'. His brothers were also creative: Henry became the manager of the National Gallery in Dublin, James wrote *The Chronicle of England* and Richard, better known as 'Dicky Doyle', was a cover designer for *Punch* magazine.

In·1868 Doyle attended the Jesuit preparatory school of Hodder in Lancashire for two years, before spending a further seven at Stonyhurst. It was here that he rejected Catholicism in favour of agnosticism. At 16 he did a further year in a Jesuit school at Feldkirch in the Austrian Tyrol (where he lapped up tales by Edgar Allan Poe) before returning to his birthplace to study medicine at Edinburgh University from 1876 to 1881.

His first published piece, a letter entitled *Gelseminum as a Poison*, appeared in the *British Medical Journal* of 20 September 1879. It detailed the effect of the drug on his own system. His first (uncredited) short story, *The Mystery of Sasassa Valley*, was published in the popular *Chambers Edinburgh Journal* in October that year.

In 1880, Doyle sailed to the Arctic Circle as an unqualified surgeon on the 400-ton Greenland whaling ship *Hope*. A year later he graduated from Edinburgh University as Bachelor of Medicine and Master of Surgery, and attempted to replicate the success of his Arctic journey by cruising the west coast of Africa on the steamship *Mayumba*. But he suffered badly from seasickness and decided it was not the life for him. It was during this time that his father Charles began to receive treatment for alcoholism and epilepsy. (He began as a fee-paying patient and was later committed to an asylum until his death in October 1893.)

Eccentric university colleague George Turnavine Budd engaged Doyle to share his medical practice in Plymouth, but later acrimoniously sacked him. Doyle (along with his brother Innes) sailed to Southsea, a suburb of Portsmouth, and started his own general medical practice at 1 Bush Villas, Elm Grove, in June 1882. Business was quiet, and he turned to writing to keep himself occupied. He joined the Portsmouth Literary and Scientific Society in winter 1883. On 6 August 1885 Doyle married Louise ('Touie') Hawkins, the sister of a patient who had died at his premises the year before. In 1887, *Beeton's Christmas Annual* published his first Sherlock Holmes novel, *A Study in Scarlet*. Two years later his first child was born, Mary Louise, and his historical novel *Micah Clarke* was published. Doyle's second Holmes novel, *The Sign of Four*, appeared in 1890.

After a brief spell in Vienna in 1891, the Doyles moved to 23 Montague Place, London, where he practised as an oculist at 2 Upper Wimpole Street, just off Harley Street. He received very few patients and decided to write short Sherlock Holmes stories for the new monthly magazine *The Strand*. With the success of these and the publication of his novel *The*

White Company, he decided to give up medicine in favour of writing.

Three months later, the Doyles rented a large house at 12 Tennison Road, South Norwood. Doyle's first son Alleyne Kingsley was born in 1892. A year later Louise, who had earlier contracted tuberculosis, was declared incurably consumptive and went to the Swiss resort of Davos to convalesce. In November 1893, Doyle joined the Society for Psychical Research, the president of which was Arthur J Balfour (who would later become prime minister), but it would be another 23 years before he began proselytising Spiritualism seriously.

Tired of Sherlock Holmes' effect on his 'serious' literary career, Doyle killed him off in *The Final Problem* in December 1893. The following year he went on an American lecture tour with his brother Innes. Doyle and his wife then spent most of 1895 in Europe before moving on to a tour of Egypt. When fighting broke out between the British and the Dervishes he volunteered as a war correspondent for *The Westminster Gazette*, giving a good account of the preparations for the campaign.

In October 1897, he and Louise moved into 'Undershaw', a house he had built in Hindhead, Surrey. Because of its height Hindhead (known as the 'English Riviera') was considered to have clean, healthy air, and Doyle hoped it would aid in Louise's recovery. But that year he met and fell in love with Jean Leckie.

The following year, he wrote two relatively unknown short stories for *The Strand* in which Holmes makes off-stage appearances. In *The Man With the Watches* (July 1898), 'a well-known criminal investigator' sends an ingenious solution to the *Daily Gazette*, while in *The Lost Special* (August 1989, later serialised by Universal in 1932) it is implied that Moriarty is the villain and Sherlock Holmes the 'amateur reasoner of some celebrity'.

In 1899 Doyle became involved in the Boer War. He sailed to South Africa in February 1900 as part of John Langman's 50-bed medical unit and worked in appalling conditions in a hospital in Bloemfontein that dealt with enteric fever. He began writing *The History of the Great Boer War* there, and also published a pro-British pamphlet entitled *The War in South Africa: Its Causes and Conduct*. In Doyle's opinion, it was this pamphlet that led to his knighthood on 9 August 1902.

Having already succumbed to public pressure and written *The Hound of the Baskervilles* in 1901 (a story set before Holmes' disappearance at the Reichenbach Falls), he finally resurrected Sherlock Holmes properly in September 1903 in a short story called *The Empty House*.

Louise died on 4 July 1906, aged 49. The same year Doyle involved himself in the case of George Edalji, a Parsee barrister whom he claimed had been wrongly accused of maiming animals. The year after, Doyle married Jean Leckie and they moved to 'Windlesham', a large house in Crowborough, East Sussex. Three children were born to this marriage: Denis Percy Stewart (1909), Adrian Malcolm (1910) and Jean Lena Annette (1912, known as Billy).

Doyle wrote more Sherlock Holmes short stories and continued campaigning against injustices. He wrote a leaflet attacking the Belgian misrule in the Congo, exposing the suffering of the natives, and investigated the case of the convicted murderer Oscar Slater. In 1909 he became president (for ten years) of the Divorce Law Reform Union. Three years later he wrote *The Lost World*, the first of three novels to feature Professor Challenger.

Aged 55 when the First World War broke out, Doyle

joined the Crowborough Company of the Sixth Royal Sussex Volunteer Regiment, but this was disbanded after a few weeks. On 2 September 1914, the Liberal politician Charles Masterman, head of the War Propaganda Bureau, asked Doyle to attend a secret meeting of Britain's leading writers to discuss ways of best promoting Britain's interests during the war. After this, Doyle went away and wrote the recruiting pamphlet *To Arms!* He then visited the Western Front, and the pamphlet *A Visit to the Three Fronts* resulted in 1916. During the war Doyle also started his six-volume *The British Campaign in France and Flanders*, completed in 1920.

In 1916, Doyle first announced his belief in Spiritualism – he claimed that the year before he had received a communication from his brother-in-law Malcolm who had died at Frameries, Belgium, in 1914. He became a passionate convert and spent the rest of his life writing and lecturing on the subject all around the world. His eldest son Alleyne was wounded at the Somme and died of pneumonia in October 1918.

Doyle believed in the Cottingley Fairies (later admitted to be a hoax), and was friends with sceptic Harry Houdini: they exchanged a series of letters on psychic matters, later published. He opened a psychic bookshop with a library and museum, and set up a psychic press which published several books.

He originally intended the short story *His Last Bow* (1917) to be the final word on the Great Detective, but nevertheless went on to write a further twelve Holmes stories over the next seven years.

By 1925 he was dividing his time between Bignell House near Minstead in the New Forest and his Crowborough abode. Following a lecture tour of Scandinavia and Holland in 1929 he developed angina pectoris and suffered a heart attack. Bedridden for several months, he died on 7 July 1930 aged 71. His last book, *The Edge of the Unknown*, had appeared a week earlier. He was buried at Crowborough but his remains were later moved – along with his wife Jean who died on 27 June 1940 – to Minstead Church. His tombstone inscription reads:

Steel True
Blade Straight
Arthur Conan Doyle
Knight
Patriot, Physician & Man of Letters

The Canon

Notes on the format:

Full title (omitting, if applicable, 'The Adventure of…' in other references).

UK and USA first publication details (with date and initials of illustrator [see below] in brackets).

The Case: A one-sentence résumé.

Date: The stated period of time in which the story takes place, occasionally as a flashback (no suppositions allowed).

Characters: Italicised ones are not directly encountered in the narrative (they usually feature in reported speech, flashbacks or passing references). Certain characters are revealed as having aliases – to preserve the twist, both names are included.

Locations: Ditto

Recorded Cases: Direct references to other canonical stories.

Unrecorded Cases: Non-canonical tales that are mentioned in passing.

Holmes: Character details, personal history, mannerisms etc.

Watson: Ditto

Elementary: Inspired deductions unrelated to the case in hand.

Quotable Quote: Holmes is the speaker unless otherwise stated.

Disguise: If any.

Problems: Inconsistencies, errors, illogical premises etc.

Observations: Background detail.

Verdict: Personal opinion about the story's merits, with a mark out of 5.

Illustrators: AB (Alec Ball), WTB (WT Benda), HMB (HM Brock), HCE (Harry C Edwards), HKE (Howard E Elcock), JRF (John Richard Flanagan), DHF (DH Friston), AG (A Gilbert), GH (Gilbert Holiday), WHH (WH Hyde), AIK (Arthur I Keller), GPN (G Patrick Nelson), SP (Sydney Paget), WP (Walter Paget), FDS (Frederic Dorr Steele), JS (Joseph Simpson), AT (Arthur Twidle), FW (Frank Wiles)

1) A Study in Scarlet

UK: *Beeton's Christmas Annual* (November 1887, DHF); USA: JB Lippincott & Co (1890)

The Case: A man's dead body lies in an empty house, with no evidence of how he died…

Characters: Stamford, Inspector Lestrade, Inspector Tobias Gregson, PC John Rance, Mrs Sawyer, Wiggins, Jefferson Hope, terrier dog, *Enoch J Drebber*, *Joseph Stangerson*, *Madame Charpentier*, *Alice Charpentier*, *Arthur Charpentier*, *John Ferrier*, *Lucy Ferrier*, *Brigham Young*, *Cowper*, *Watson's dog.*

Locations: Private hotel, Strand; Criterion Bar, Piccadilly Circus; 'The Holborn' restaurant; chemical lab in St Bartholomew's Hospital; 221B Baker Street; 3 Lauriston Gardens, Brixton; 46 Audley Court, Kennington Park Gate; unnamed police station; *Charpentier's Boarding Establishment, Torquay Terrace, Camberwell; Halliday's Private Hotel, Little George Street; Sierra Blanco, North America; Salt Lake City and its environs, Utah; Cleveland, Ohio; Euston Station, London.*

Unrecorded Cases: Von Bischoff of Frankfurt, Mason of

Bradford, the notorious Muller, Lefevre and Leturier of Montpellier, Samson of New Orleans, Van Jansen of Utrecht (in 1834), the Ratcliff Highway murders, Dolsky of Odessa.

Holmes: Is said by Stamford to be 'well up' in anatomy, a 'first-class' chemist with 'a passion for definite and exact knowledge'. He is cold-bloodedly scientific: he beats corpses with a stick to observe bruising and dabbles with poisons. Has just discovered a re-agent precipitated by haemoglobin that will revolutionise the detection of bloodstains. Admits to long periods of sulking. Plays the violin very well (and uses it to express his mood swings) and is sensitive to flattery. Is quiet and regular in his habits, goes to bed before ten and is out before Watson rises in the morning. Over six-feet tall, lean, sharp-eyed, square-jawed and hawk-nosed. Claims to be ignorant of the workings of the solar system and hasn't heard of Thomas Carlyle (1795–1881). A boxer, swordsman and single-stick expert. (This last is a stick fitted with a handguard and used in fencing.) Has an immense knowledge of nineteenth century crime cases and has written a magazine article called 'The Book of Life', illustrating the deductive process through observation. Calls himself the world's only consulting detective and refers disdainfully to Scotland Yard in the same breath as Edgar Allan Poe and Emile Gaboriau's fictional detectives, Dupin and Lecoq. He keeps a tape-measure and a large magnifying glass in his pocket and chatters to himself as he looks for clues. Has written a monograph on cigar ash. He thinks music affects us because, according to Darwin, it predates language. Outdoors he wears an ulster (a long loose overcoat) and a cravat. When commenting on Lestrade and Gregson, he quotes French poet and critic Nicolas Boileau-Despréaux (1636–1711): 'An idiot always finds an even bigger idiot to admire him.'

Watson: In 1878, he took a Doctor of Medicine degree at the University of London, went on an army surgeons' course at Netley and then joined the Fifth Northumberland Fusiliers in Kandahar, Afghanistan. He received a shoulder wound from a Jezail bullet at the Battle of Maiwand (July 1880), suffered enteric fever at Peshawar, and was sent back to Portsmouth. He spends some time in London but is running out of money. He suffers from war fatigue, gets up in the small hours and is extremely lazy. At this early stage he doesn't suspect Holmes of drug-taking. The bull pup he mentions and that is never seen again *may* be the bull terrier that is humanely put down by Holmes.

Elementary: Holmes deduces that Watson comes from Afghanistan, and that the messenger is a retired Marine sergeant.

Quotable Quote: 'There's the scarlet thread of murder running though the colourless skein of life, and our duty is to unravel it…'

Problems: Holmes' revolutionary bloodstain test is never referred to again. Utah and the Rio Grande are incorrectly sited. Jefferson Hope would be unlikely to return to 221B Baker Street after his accomplice had previously visited it. Holmes claims never to have heard of Thomas Carlyle, yet quotes from his *Frederick the Great* ('They say that genius is an infinite capacity for taking pains').

Observations: Inspired by Robert Louis Stevenson's *The Dynamiter* (1885), Doyle worked on this story (originally called *A Tangled Skein*) from March to April 1886 at Southsea, Hants. He based his detective on Dr Joseph Bell, a teacher of medicine during his time at Edinburgh University. An admirer of Poe's Auguste Dupin and Gaboriau's Monsieur Lecoq, he toyed with the idea of calling his detective Sherrinford Holmes before settling on the name we are familiar with. 'Sherlock' was possibly based on prominent violinist Alfred Sherlock, while American medical pioneer Oliver Wendell Holmes may have inspired the surname. 'Ormond Sacker' became 'John H Watson' (a Dr James Watson was already known to Doyle). After touting the manuscript to various publishers, he was eventually paid the flat fee of £25 by Ward, Lock & Co, publishers of *Beeton's Christmas Annual*, founded 27 years earlier by Samual Orchart Beeton (husband of famous cook Isabella). Doyle wrote the story without visiting America; his information about Mormonism was gleaned in part from the *Encyclopaedia Britannica* and various newspaper articles. He copied Gaboriau's device of splitting a novel in two, with a solved crime followed by an adventure novella. There was no Lauriston Gardens in London, but Lauriston Place in Edinburgh was the road nearest to the house in which Doyle lived. Some have claimed that the story was based on the real-life case of the disappearance of a German baker, Urban Napoleon Stanger, on 12 November 1881 in London's East End. The Baker Street Irregulars are only referred to as 'street Arabs'.

The Latin quotation that closes the book is from *Satires* Book I:1:67 by lyric poet Horace (65–8 BC) and is translated thus: 'The crowd hiss me, but I applaud myself at home, as soon as I contemplate the money in my chest.'

A Study in Scarlet was published as a 'shilling shocker' by Ward, Lock & Co, with naïve illustrations by Doyle's father Charles (who gave Holmes a beard). Later editions featured illustrations by George Hutchinson. The book was presented free with *The Windsor Magazine* in December 1895, illustrated by James Greig.

Verdict: A disappointing debut for the Great Detective, this is essentially a padded short story (most of Part 2 being redundant) in which Holmes appears only briefly. But he is clearly a tremendous creation – a dynamic character far superior to the romanticised melodrama in which he finds himself, he springs fully formed (if oddly hale and hearty) from the page. 4/5

2) The Sign of Four

UK and USA: *Lippincott's Monthly Magazine* (February 1890)
The Case: A mysterious benefactor, who has been sending an orphan a pearl every year, at last promises to reveal his true identity…
Date: See 'Problems'.

Characters: Inspector Athelney Jones, Mary Morstan, Mrs Cecil Forrester, Thaddeus and Bartholomew Sholto, Williams and McMurdo, Mrs Bernstone, Lal Rao, Jonathan Small, Sherman, Mordecai Smith, Mrs Smith, Jim and Jack Smith, Wiggins, Mrs Hudson, Tonga, *Captain Arthur Morstan, Major John Sholto, Sergeant John Holder, Abel White, Mahomet Singh, Abdullah Kahn, Dost Akbar, Achmet, Dr Somerton.*

Locations: 221B Baker Street; Lyceum Theatre, London; house near Cold Harbour Lane; Pondicherry Lodge, Upper Norwood; 3 Pinchin Lane, Lambeth; Broderick & Nelson's timber yard, Nine Elms; Smith's Wharf, Lambeth; Mrs Cecil Forrester's house, Camberwell; Westminster Stairs; Jacobson's Yard, SE1; Plumstead Marshes, SE18; *Indigo plantation, Muttra, India; Agra Fort, India; Hope Town, Blair Island, Andaman Islands, Indian Ocean.*

Recorded Case: A Study in Scarlet.

Unrecorded Cases: Riga in 1857 and St Louis in 1871 (both concerning wills), Mrs Cecil Forrester's 'domestic complication', a woman who poisoned three children for their insurance money, parallel cases in India and Senegambia, the Bishopsgate jewel case.

Holmes: Is described as a young man. Has been taking a seven per cent solution of morphine or cocaine three times a day for many months. He objects to Watson's romanticism in *A Study in Scarlet*. Smokes a briar-root pipe. Thinks French detective François le Villard is deficient in exact knowledge. Has written several monographs – *Upon the Distinction Between the Ashes of the Various Tobaccos* and others on the tracing of footsteps and the influences of a trade upon the form of the hand. Has an 'extraordinary genius for minutiae', according to Watson. He is egotistical and vain. Thinks of clients as 'units' and doesn't get emotionally involved. He carries a revolver if he thinks the situation calls for it. Keeps a 'double lens' and a tape-measure on his person. He once took part in amateur boxing. He is now familiar (cf. *A Study in Scarlet*) with the writings of Jean Paul (Friedrich) Richter (1763–1825) and Thomas Carlyle. Idleness exhausts him, but smoking helps him think. Considers William Winwood Reade's *The Martyrdom of Man* (1872) one of the most remarkable books ever written. Is interested in miracle plays, medieval pottery, Stradivarius violins, Ceylon Buddhism and futuristic warships. Thinks women are untrustworthy, dislikes love because it is emotional, and would never marry because it would cloud his judgement. Has never shot at anyone before. Quotes Goethe when referring to Athelney Jones ('We are used to the fact that people make fun of the things they don't understand') and later to himself ('It is too bad that nature made you just a human, since there was material to make a worthy man and a jester').

Watson: Has not got over his Afghan experience yet. He has an older brother, his father has been dead many years and he has known women of many nations. Has a weak bank balance.

Visited Ballarat. Keeps an old service revolver in his desk. Drinks Beaune (a red burgundy wine) and objects to Holmes' drug habit.

Elementary: Holmes knows Watson has been to Wigmore Street post office to dispatch a telegram, and deduces the owner of a watch Watson has recently been sent.

Quotable Quote: 'I never guess. It is a shocking habit – destructive to the logical faculty.'

Problems: The narrative begins on 8 July 1888; then suddenly we are told it is September with accompanying autumnal weather conditions. But later Holmes says it will be light at 3am (!), implying midsummer again.

Watson's war wound has travelled from his shoulder to his leg. Watson sees Holmes leaving dressed as a sailor, yet is surprised when he is later revealed... dressed as a sailor. Andamanese Negrito pygmies are peaceful, not cannibals, and have an average height of over four feet. Crocodiles are not known for amputating limbs cleanly. The Indian members of the Four are supposed to be Sikhs, but two have Moslem names and Mahomet Singh has an impossible combination of Moslem and Sikh.

Disguise: An elderly sea dog.

Observations: In August 1889 Doyle and Oscar Wilde were commissioned by JM Stoddard to write stories for the American magazine *Lippincott's*. Wilde penned *The Picture of Dorian Gray*, while Doyle revived Sherlock Holmes in *The Sign of the Four*, taking less than a month on the manuscript. He received £100 for the magazine serial rights. It was later issued as a book by Spencer Blackett (with one illustration by Charles Kerr) for which the title was shortened to *The Sign of Four*, remaining so in all UK editions.

Verdict: Ultimately one long chase, this may be more adventure yarn than detective story, but it's undeniably exciting. Doyle has learnt the lesson of *A Study in Scarlet* and the explanatory flashback takes up less than one chapter. Holmes displays more of the characteristics we expect here – detached coldness and a reliance on cocaine to stave off depression – and Watson's romance is nicely handled. The implicit racism is unfortunate, but at least Watson rails against Holmes' sexism. 5/5

3) A Scandal in Bohemia

UK: *The Strand Magazine* (July 1891, SP)

The Case: A king wishes to reclaim compromising letters he sent to an opera singer...

Date: 20–22 March 1888.

Characters: Wilhelm Gottsreich Sigismond von Ormstein, Irene Adler (later Norton), Godfrey Norton, Mrs Turner, Mary Jane, *Clotilde Lothman von Saxe-Meningen.*

Locations: 221B Baker Street; Briony Lodge, Serpentine's Avenue, St John's Wood; *Church of St Monica, Edgware Road; Gross & Hankey's, Regent Street.*

Recorded Case: A Study in Scarlet.

Unrecorded Cases: Trepoff murder at Odessa, Atkinson brothers at Trincomalee, mission for the Dutch royal family, Darlington Substitution Scandal, Arnsworth Castle business.

Holmes: Has a bohemian soul but is still concerned about receiving the correct payment for his work. Keeps a case of cigars and a *Continental Gazetteer.* Walks arm in arm with Watson and calls him 'my Boswell'. Likes cold beef and beer.

Watson: Has left 221B Baker Street for a London practice, marriage having separated him from Holmes's company. Is already used to the latter's disguises.

Elementary: Holmes deduces that Watson has got wet recently and that he has a clumsy servant girl.

Quotable Quote: 'You see, but you do not observe. The distinction is clear.'

Disguises: A drunken groom and a nonconformist clergyman.

Problems: Holmes knew time was running out so why didn't he put a watch on Irene Adler's house? It's unlikely a cab could get from St John's Wood to the Edgware Road via a Regent Street shop before another one going straight there. The date clashes with the previous story. It is never explained how Holmes gathered up so many accomplices. The housekeeper is called Mrs Turner (the same thing happens in the manuscript of *The Empty House* – it seems Doyle couldn't remember the name he had previously used).

Observations: Established in January 1891 by George Newnes, the monthly *Strand Magazine* broke new ground by publishing complete short stories featuring recurring characters. Thinking Sherlock Holmes would be an ideal choice for this fledgling genre, Doyle's agent AP Watt sent two stories to editor Herbert Greenhough Smith – this one and *The Red-Headed League.* Another four swiftly followed, for which Doyle was paid approximately £200 in total. Walter Paget had been chosen to illustrate the story (Newnes' policy was to print a picture on every page), but his brother Sidney was commissioned in error. Walter then became Sidney's model for Holmes while art school student Alfred Morris Butler (who bore a strong resemblance to Doyle) posed for Watson. This first story mirrors at least two real-life royalty liaisons: singer Ludmilla Hubel and Ludwig I of Bavaria, and Lillie Langtry and the Prince of Wales (later Edward VII). A gasogene was the precursor of the soda siphon.

Verdict: A lightweight domestic melodrama played for laughs, it lacks a certain something. But its *Mission:Impossible*-style plot

is entertaining, as is Holmes's offhand approach to royalty.
3/5

4) The Red-Headed League

UK: *The Strand Magazine* (August 1891, SP)
The Case: A pawnbroker is mystified as to why his lucrative part-time job has suddenly ended...
Date: 9–10 October 1890.
Characters: Jabez Wilson, Vincent Spaulding, John Clay, Inspector Peter Jones, Merryweather, *Ezekiah Hopkins, Duncan Ross, William Morris.*
Locations: 221B Baker Street; St James's Hall, Piccadilly; Saxe-Coburg Square, off Farringdon Street; City and Suburban Bank, Farringdon Street; *4 Pope's Court, Fleet Street*; *17 King Edward Street, St Paul's.*
Recorded Cases: A Case of Identity, The Sign of Four.
Holmes: Has written about tattoos. Says Watson has embellished his cases. Has a good sense of humour. Judges the complexity of a case by the number of pipes he smokes (this one is a three-pipe problem). Prefers German music when feeling introspective. Is a gifted composer. Plays bridge or whist. Carries a hunting crop. Quotes Gustave Flaubert.
Watson: Lives to the south of Hyde Park where he finds his medical practice unabsorbing.
Elementary: Deduces Jabez Wilson is a manual labourer, Freemason, snuff-taker, has recently written a great deal and has visited China.
Quotable Quote: 'My life is spent in one long effort to escape from the commonplaces of existence.'
Problems: Holmes mentions Mary Sutherland's case, which isn't until the next story. The date is 9 October 1890 yet Wilson's

advert appeared on 27 April, 'two months ago'. Coburg Square alternates with Saxe-Coburg Square. Athelney Jones appears to have changed his name to Peter. Getting Wilson out of his pawnbroker's is unnecessary as Wilson already knows Spaulding spends hours in the cellar. In fact, having him back in the shop during the robbery is illogical – that's the one time he should be absent.

Verdict: Amusing diversions ('a manufactory of artificial kneecaps') colour this weird but intriguing tale of redheads and encyclopaedia-copying. 4/5

5) A Case of Identity

UK: *The Strand Magazine* (September 1891, SP)

The Case: A retiring office clerk mysteriously vanishes just before his wedding...

Characters: Mary Sutherland, James Windibank, page, *Hosmer Angel*, *Mr Hardy*.

Locations: 221B Baker Street; *St Saviour's, near King's Cross*; *31 Lyon Place, Camberwell*; *Westhouse & Marbank, Fenchurch Street*.

Recorded Case: A Scandal in Bohemia.

Unrecorded Cases: The Dundas separation case, an intricate matter from Marseilles, Mr Etherege's disappearance, similar cases in Andover in 1877 and The Hague the previous year.

Holmes: Uses an amethyst-inlaid snuffbox given to him by the King of Bohemia, and wears a ring from the reigning family of Holland (see *A Scandal in Bohemia*). Has 10 or 12 cases currently on the go. Smokes an old black clay pipe. Observes people's sleeves, thumbnails and bootlaces. Has studied the typewriter and its relation to crime and wants to write a monograph on it.

Elementary: Deduces that Mary Sutherland is a short-sighted typist.

Quotable Quote: 'My first glance is always at a woman's sleeve. In a man it is perhaps better first to take the knee of the trouser.'

Problem: Holmes says the final quotation is from the works of fourteenth-century Persian lyric poet Hafiz – it isn't (no one knows where it's from).

Observations: Holmes solves the case without venturing outside his rooms, and a page (a 'boy in buttons') appears for the first time. This story was written (and set) before *The Red-Headed League*, but the latter was considered stronger and was published first.

Verdict: Deduct two points for the preposterous twist, but the notion of such long-term fidelity is charming and having Holmes assume the role of a moral guardian is very effective. 3/5

6) The Boscombe Valley Mystery

UK: *The Strand Magazine* (October 1891, SP)

The Case: In a small West Country district, a young man has been accused of murdering his father...

Characters: John Turner, Alice Turner, Inspector Lestrade, Charles McCarthy, James McCarthy, William Crowder, Patience Moran, Dr Willows.

Locations: Watson's medical practice; Paddington Station; Hereford Arms, Ross, Herts; Hatherley Farm, Herts; Boscombe Pool, Herts.

Holmes: Wears a long grey travelling cloak and a close-fitting cloth cap, and at Boscombe he also has a waterproof. Describes himself and Watson as middle-aged. Reads Petrarch and George Meredith (1828–1909). Exhibits lust for the chase, and answers questions with an impatient snarl when concentrating.

Watson: Is very strict about shaving properly.

Elementary: Deduces Watson's bedroom window is on the right-hand side.

Quotable Quote: 'The more featureless and commonplace a crime is, the more difficult it is to bring it home.'

Problem: In the newspaper article, the 'Witness' and 'Coroner' directions disappear three quarters of the way through.

Observations: The first case not to feature 221B Baker Street. The story was inspired by Henry Beresford Garrett, one of a gang who robbed the Bank of Victoria in the Australian town of Ballarat in October 1854, stealing £14,300. Sidney Paget drew Holmes' famous deerstalker and ulster for the first time, although the former is not mentioned by Doyle.

Verdict: The first story set outside London, this is rather a plodding narrative with little incident. Holmes and Watson never even meet the victim of injustice. 2/5

7) The Five Orange Pips

UK: *The Strand Magazine* (November 1891, SP)

The Case: A man receives an odd gift which he knows is a portent of doom…

Date: Late September 1887.

Characters: John Openshaw, *Joseph Openshaw, Colonel Elias Openshaw, Mr Fordham, Major Freebody, Major Prendergast, Captain James Calhoun.*

Locations: 221B Baker Street; *Colonel Elias' house, Horsham, Sussex; landing stage near Waterloo Bridge; Lone Star barque.*

Recorded Cases: A Study in Scarlet, The Sign of Four.

Unrecorded Cases: The adventure of the Paradol Chamber, the Amateur Mendicant Society, the loss of the British barque *Sophie Anderson*, the Grice Patersons on the island of Uffa, the

Camberwell poisoning case, Major Prendergast in the Tankerville Club Scandal.

Holmes: Has been unable to solve some cases, and others are only partially solved. Has been beaten four times, once (probably) by Irene Adler, thrice by unknown men. Watson is his only friend. Cross-indexes all his crime records. Thinks *The Sign of Four* is the most fantastic case they've yet worked on. Compares his deduction process to that of influential French palaeontologist Georges Cuvier (1769–1832).

Watson: Enjoys Clark Russell's seafaring tales. Still remembers list of Holmes' limitations from *A Study in Scarlet*.

Quotable Quote: '…a man should keep his little brain attic stocked with all the furniture that he is likely to use, and the rest he can put away in the lumber-room of his library…'

Problems: Holmes has no reason to believe that more than one murderer is involved. Doyle's original manuscript states that Mary Watson was visiting her mother – who had died before *The Sign of Four*. This was amended to 'aunt' for the UK edition, although the American version remains unchanged.

Observations: A rare case in which Holmes is seen to fail.

Verdict: Beginning and ending with autumnal gales, this is an unusual tale in which the villains receive their come-uppance by divine, rather than legal, judgement. The gales' presence permeates the narrative – a sign of uncontrollable 'elemental forces' – to the extent that even the Great Detective bows down to a higher, more mysterious, power. One of the few Sherlock Holmes stories to work on more than one level. 5/5

8) The Man with the Twisted Lip

UK: *The Strand Magazine* (December 1891, SP)
The Case: A City businessman appears to have been murdered

by a scarred beggar...

Date: 19–20 June 1889.

Characters: Mary Watson, Isa Whitney, Inspector Bradstreet, Kate Whitney, Neville and Mrs St Clair, Hugh Boone, *Elias Whitney, unnamed Lascar, Inspector Barton.*

Locations: Watson's house; Bar of Gold opium den, Upper Swandam Lane, EC3; The Cedars, near Lee, Kent; Bow Street Magistrates Court, WC2; *Aberdeen Shipping Company, Fresno Street, EC3.*

Holmes: Is skilled at driving a horse and trap (like his brother Mycroft in *The Final Problem*). Wears a blue dressing gown and can spend all night sitting cross-legged and smoking if mulling over a problem. Has strong-set aquiline features.

Disguise: An old opium addict.

Quotable Quote: '...it is better to learn wisdom late, than never to learn it at all.'

Problems: Watson's wife calls her husband 'James' – it may be a pet name, but would she use it in the presence of a third party? Hugh Boone is apprehended in the City of London and so would not be taken to Bow Street police station.

Observations: It has similarities to William Makepeace Thackeray's tale of Mr Altamont in his *Yellowplush Papers.*

Verdict: A satire on charity and a sly dig at the perils of capitalism, this is an amusing tale that sees Holmes unmasking the culprit with the aid of a wet sponge! 5/5

9) The Adventure of the Blue Carbuncle

UK: *The Strand Magazine* (January 1892, SP)

The Case: A fabulous jewel has been stolen from a countess' hotel room...

Characters: Peterson, James Ryder, Henry Baker, Windigate,

Breckinridge, *The Countess of Morcar, John Horner, Catherine Cusack, Inspector Bradstreet, Maggie Oakshott, Maudsley*.

Locations: 221B Baker Street; Alpha Inn, Bloomsbury; Covent Garden Market; *Junction of Goodge Street and Tottenham Court Road*; *Hotel Cosmopolitan*; *117 Brixton Road*; *Maudsley's house, Kilburn*.

Recorded Cases: A Scandal in Bohemia, A Case of Identity, The Man with the Twisted Lip.

Unrecorded Cases: Two murders, a vitriol throwing, suicide and several robberies attend the history of the Blue Carbuncle.

Holmes: Wears a purple dressing gown. Believes the size of the head indicates intelligence, and that gemstones are a magnet to criminals. Laughs in a hearty but noiseless fashion. Refers to a mugging as a 'whimsical little incident'.

Elementary: Deduces a man's personality and lifestyle from his hat.

Quotable Quote: 'Send him to gaol now, and you make him a gaolbird for life. Besides, it is the season of forgiveness.'

Problems: A carbuncle is a red stone (usually a garnet) cut in a particular way, not a crystallised carbon like a diamond. The story ends with John Horner still wrongfully accused.

Observations: Doyle was paid £300 in total for this and the next five stories.

Verdict: A sort of literary 'Christmas special', this is a deliberately comic tale with more than its fair share of humour. Even Holmes is not above cracking the odd pun. 4/5

10) The Adventure of the Speckled Band

UK: *The Strand Magazine* (February 1892, SP)
The Case: A woman dies of fright in a locked room, and her sister thinks she'll be next...

Date: Early April 1883.

Characters: Helen Stoner, Dr Grimesby Roylott, *Julia Stoner*, *Honoria Westphail, Percy Armitage.*

Locations: 221B Baker Street; Stoke Moran Manor House, Stoke Moran, Surrey; Crown Inn, Stoke Moran, Surrey.

Unrecorded Case: Mrs Farintosh and the opal tiara (pre-1880).

Holmes: Is usually a late riser. Can straighten a steel poker. Thinks a revolver and a toothbrush are the only items needed when journeying to a crime scene.

Watson: Has been chronicling Holmes' exploits for eight years, totalling 70 cases. Is a bachelor at the time of this case and is regular in his habits.

Elementary: Deduces Helen Stoner's modes of transport to Baker Street.

Quotable Quote: 'Ah, me! It's a wicked world, and when a clever man turns his brain to crime it is the worst of all.'

Problems: There are no baboons in India. The swamp adder is an invented species (although the North American massasauga comes close), and snakes are deaf and dislike milk. A snakebite would have been easily observed by a coroner.

Observations: Reference is made to real-life poisoners William Palmer (hanged 1856) and Edward William Pritchard (hanged 1863). Both were physicians, but despite what Holmes says, neither were 'at the head' of their profession.

Verdict: A genuinely creepy and well-constructed mystery, its solution is logical yet unexpected – a perfect combination. 5/5

11) The Adventure of the Engineer's Thumb

UK: *The Strand Magazine* (March 1892, SP)

The Case: An engineer escapes from counterfeiters with the loss of his thumb...

Date: Summer 1889.

Characters: Train guard, Victor Hatherley, Dr Becher, Inspector Bradstreet, plain-clothes policeman, stationmaster, *Colonel Lysander Stark, Ferguson, Elise.*

Locations: Watson's house; 221B Baker Street; *16a Victoria Street*; *house in Eyford, Berks.*

Unrecorded Case: Colonel Warburton's madness.

Holmes: Has a pre-breakfast pipe consisting of the remains of the previous day's tobacco. Enjoys a hearty breakfast of bacon and eggs.

Watson: Has been married for a short time and has a steadily increasing practice near Paddington Station. Still visits Holmes and encourages him to visit him and his wife.

Problems: It is not made clear whether 'Lysander Stark' and 'Mr Ferguson' are aliases for Fritz and Dr Becher (or vice versa), and the role of Elise is unclear. It is prescient of Holmes to ask about the horse's condition before he is told of the long journey. There is some confusion as to how Hatherley's thumb was severed: in the *Strand* text he is hanging by his *fingers* only (his thumbs are under the sill), and this is reflected by Paget's illustration. Why was the massive (and heavy) press installed on the first floor and not the ground?

Observations: The story, a replay of a similar one by Wilkie Collins, is penned by Watson two years after the event. It is the only case the doctor has initiated.

Verdict: Holmes exhibits few of his detective powers in this macabre little misadventure. Its lack of resolution and shadowy villains are frustrating. 2/5

12) The Adventure of the Noble Bachelor

UK: The Strand Magazine (April 1892, SP)

The Case: A newly titled bride disappears at her wedding breakfast...

Date: Autumn 1887 (a few weeks before Watson's marriage).
Characters: Lord Robert Walsingham de Vere St Simon, Inspector Lestrade, Mr & Mrs Francis Hay Moulton, page-boy, *Lord Backwater, Hatty Doran, Aloysius Doran, Duchess of Balmoral, Lord Eustace and Lady Clara St Simon, Lady Alicia Whittington, Flora Millar, Alice.*

Locations: 221B Baker Street; *St George's, Hanover Square; house at Lancaster Gate; McQuire's camp, near the Rockies; San Francisco; miners' camp, New Mexico; a Northumberland Avenue hotel; 226 Gordon Square.*

Unrecorded Cases: A Grosvenor Square furniture van, the King of Scandinavia, parallel cases in Aberdeen and Munich.

Holmes: Dislikes snobbery, likes Americans. Enjoys a whisky and soda with a cigar. Quotes Henry Thoreau (1817–62).

Quotable Quote: '...I am one of those who believe that the folly of a monarch and the blundering of a Minister in far gone years will not prevent our children from being some day citizens of the same worldwide country under a flag which shall be a quartering of the Union Jack with the Stars and Stripes.'

Problems: Watson married Mary Morstan after July 1888 (see *The Sign of Four*) – this story is set 'a few weeks before', but in 1887. Dumping unweighted clothes in the Serpentine is a poor way of disposing of the evidence – burning or burying them would be more effective. Frank's return from the dead is not explained.

Observations: A case with parallels to *A Scandal in Bohemia*, this is another story that takes place entirely within 221B Baker Street.

Verdict: Less an upper-crust romantic triangle, more a dialogue-heavy sermon by Doyle on Anglo-American relations. 2/5

13) The Adventure of the Beryl Coronet

UK: *The Strand Magazine* (May 1892, SP)

The Case: A banker's reputation is at stake when a famous diadem goes missing...

Characters: Alexander Holder, Mary Holder, *Arthur Holder, Sir George Burnwell, Lucy Parr, Francis Prosper.*

Locations: 221B Baker Street; Fairbank, Streatham.

Holmes: Is not above doing a deal with a criminal.

Disguise: A common loafer.

Quotable Quote: 'It is an old maxim of mine that when you have excluded the impossible, whatever remains, however improbable, must be the truth.'

Observations: Although the year is unknown (we are only told it is February), the story must have happened before Watson's marriage, because he is still sharing rooms with Holmes. Although the client's identity is kept secret, a possible contender could be Prince Alfred, Duke of Edinburgh, and second son of Queen Victoria.

Problem: Although the division between royal and state property can be a grey area, it is unlikely a coronet could legally be used as security for a loan.

Verdict: Doyle may already be borrowing ideas from previous stories (notably *The Blue Carbuncle* and *The Sign of Four*), but the main protagonist's predicament is engaging, and the resultant clue-solving well described. 4/5

14) The Adventure of the Copper Beeches

UK: *The Strand Magazine* (June 1892, SP)

The Case: A highly paid governess fears for her safety in an eccentric country house...

Characters: Violet Hunter, Jephro Rucastle, Mrs Toller, country surgeon, *Colonel Spence Munro, Miss Stoper, Mrs Rucastle, Alice Rucastle, Mr Toller, Master Rucastle, Fowler.*

Recorded Cases: A Scandal in Bohemia, A Case of Identity, The Man with the Twisted Lip, The Noble Bachelor, The Blue Carbuncle.

Locations: 221B Baker Street; The Copper Beeches, Southampton Road, near Winchester, Hants; The Black Swan, High Street, Winchester; *Montague Place, WC1; Westaway's, West End.*

Holmes: Smokes a long cherrywood pipe when he is in an argumentative mood. Feels his time is being wasted with trivial cases. Analyses acetones. Has devised seven separate explanations for the mystery before even arriving at the crime scene.

Watson: Is repelled by Holmes' egotism.

Quotable Quote: 'It is my belief, Watson, founded upon my experience, that the lowest and vilest alleys in London do not present a more dreadful record of sin than does the smiling and beautiful countryside.'

Problems: Violet's dress is 'a peculiar shade of blue' as well as 'a sort of beige' – but beige means 'the yellowish-grey colour of undyed and unbleached wool'. It was a bit incompetent to give Violet a key to the all-important drawer containing a lock of Alice Rucastle's hair.

Observations: Montague Place was where Doyle lived when he worked as an ophthalmologist. The idea for this story allegedly came from the author's mother; and she persuaded him not to kill Holmes in it, as was his original intention. Holmes mentions a sister, but this is probably a figure of speech.

Verdict: A weak tale, the chief interest is its foreshadowing of *The Hound of the Baskervilles* with its use of a giant dog. Characterisation is in places sketchy, with the evil boy not even receiving a name. But Violet Hunter is a splendid creation: a feisty, intelligent young woman who would have made an ideal companion for Holmes. 3/5

15) The Adventure of Silver Blaze

UK: *The Strand Magazine* (December 1892, SP); USA: *Harper's Weekly* (25 February 1893, WHH)

The Case: A champion racehorse is stolen on the eve of an important race...

Characters: Colonel Ross, Inspector Gregory, Silas Brown, groom, stable lad, Silver Blaze, *John Straker, Mrs Straker, Fitzroy Simpson, Lord Blackwater, Ned Hunter, Edith Baxter, William Darbyshire, Madame Darbyshire.*

Locations: 221B Baker Street; King's Pyland stables, Dartmoor, Devon; Tavistock Station, Dartmoor, Devon; Capleton stables, Dartmoor, Devon; Wessex Cup racecourse, near Winchester, Hants.

Holmes: Smokes strong black tobacco. In the country he wears an ear-flapped travelling cap. Uses his imagination and then looks for clues to support it. Bets on horses. Delays revealing the facts to Ross because of his rudeness.

Watson: Smokes a cigar.

Quotable Quote:

Gregory: 'Is there any other point to which you would wish to draw my attention?'

Holmes: 'To the curious incident of the dog in the night-time.'

Gregory: 'The dog did nothing in the night-time.'

Holmes: 'That was the curious incident.'

Elementary: Holmes deduces the train's speed using telegraph posts.

Problems: It is debatable that Ross wouldn't recognise his own horse, despite its disguised markings. Pullmans had never been used on the West of England line, and the South Western's London terminus is not Victoria. Doyle was to later write that, 'the racing detail in *Silver Blaze* is very faulty'.

Observations: This is the first of Doyle's second dozen stories for *The Strand*, for which he was paid £1,000 in total. He would return to Dartmoor in *The Hound of the Baskervilles*.

Verdict: Atmospherically written, although the plot itself is rather on the dull side. 3/5

16) The Adventure of the Cardboard Box

UK: *The Strand Magazine* (January 1893, SP); USA: *Harper's Weekly* (14 January 1893, WHH)

The Case: A middle-aged spinster receives two severed ears in the post...

Characters: Susan Cushing, Inspector Lestrade, doctor, *Sarah Cushing, Mary Cushing, Jim Browner, Algar, Inspector Montgomery, Alec Fairbairn.*

Locations: 221B Baker Street; Cross Street, Croydon; New Street, Wallington; police station, Croydon; *Albert Dock, Liverpool; Shadwell police station; Liverpool; New Brighton, Liverpool.*

Recorded Cases: A Study in Scarlet, The Sign of Four.

Unrecorded Case: Aldridge who helped in the affair of the bogus laundry.

Holmes: Purchased a Stradivarius for the bargain price of 55 shillings at a Jewish pawnbroker's in Tottenham Court Road.

Knows lots of anecdotes about Paganini. Has written two short monographs in an edition of the *Anthropological Review* on peculiarities of the human ear. Reads Poe (cf. *A Study in Scarlet*).

Quotable Quote: 'What is the meaning of it, Watson?... What object is served by this circle of misery and violence and fear? It must tend to some end, or else our universe is ruled by chance, which is unthinkable.'

Problems: 'Brain fever' (a catch-all for nervous trouble, shock etc.) is used to create an artificial hiatus and allow Holmes to investigate. Watson was only ten at the time of the American Civil War, so is unlikely to feel strongly about it.

Observations: Doyle did not include this story in the book version of *The Memoirs* for two reasons – he considered it too shocking, and it exposed the seamier side of infidelity. (Royal infidelity was tolerated as a literary cliché, but the common variety was frowned upon.) 24 years later it was included in the penultimate collection *His Last Bow*. But Doyle transferred the story's opening 'mind-reading' scene, with minor changes, to *The Resident Patient* (replacing its original introduction) when it was issued in *The Memoirs* (1894).

Verdict: An engrossing mystery solved by a logical process of deduction. The actual murder is very atmospherically described. 5/5

17) The Adventure of the Yellow Face

UK: *The Strand Magazine* (February 1893, SP); USA: *Harper's Weekly* (11 February 1893, WHH)

The Case: A husband is concerned that his wife is seeing someone else...

Characters: Page-boy, Grant Munro, Effie Munro, Lucy Hebron, Scotchwoman, *John Hebron*.

Locations: Regent's or Hyde Park, London; 221B Baker Street; *house and cottage in Norbury; Crystal Palace; Atlanta, Georgia.*
Recorded Case: The Second Stain.

Holmes: Is a fine boxer but seldom takes exercise for its own sake. Still uses cocaine occasionally. Believes pipes, watches and shoelaces show a person's individuality.

Elementary: Deduces a man's character and habits from his pipe.

Quotable Quote: 'Watson… if it should ever strike you that I am getting a little overconfident in my powers, or giving less pains to a case than it deserves, kindly whisper "Norbury" in my ear, and I shall be infinitely obliged to you.' (Norbury being the place where he got things wrong.)

Problems: Grant Munro's wife repeatedly calls him 'Jack'. (Perhaps Doyle is making the point that wives adopt pet names for their husbands, as Mary Watson did in *The Man with the Twisted Lip*.) Interracial marriages were illegal in Georgia. In the American Doubleday edition, the yellow face becomes 'chalky white' (although the title remains unchanged). Why didn't Grant Munro notice that the photograph he commissioned of his wife was missing?

Verdict: The main villain of this story is the appalling racism of Victorian England. And although Doyle ends the narrative on an optimistic note, the unconscious xenophobia of all (including, it must be said, the author) is particularly unsavoury. Interesting, I suppose, to see Holmes getting things totally wrong for once, but hard to like. 2/5

18) The Adventure of the Stockbroker's Clerk

UK: *The Strand Magazine* (March 1893, SP); USA: *Harper's Weekly* (11 March 1893, WHH)

The Case: A City worker grows suspicious when two employers turn out to be the same man in disguise...

Characters: Hall Pycroft, Arthur and Harry Pinner, the Beddington brothers, *Mary Watson, landlady, Parker, Sergeant Tuson, Constable Pollock, Dr Farquhar.*

Locations: Watson's practice, Paddington; Franco-Midland Hardware Company Ltd, 126B Corporation Street, Birmingham; *Coxon and Woodhouse, Drapers' Gardens; Mawson and Williams, Lombard Street; 17 Potter's Terrace, Hampstead; New Street hotel, Birmingham.*

Recorded Case: The Sign of Four.

Watson: Shortly after his marriage, he buys a failing medical practice in the Paddington district, which has now become very busy (he and his neighbour cover for each other). At the drop of a hat he rushes off with Holmes, so must have a very understanding wife. Thinks Cockneys make the best sportsmen and athletes.

Elementary: Deduces Watson has had a cold, and that his practice is more successful than his neighbour's.

Quotable Quote: 'I am afraid that I rather give myself away when I explain... Results without causes are much more impressive.'

Problems: It is never explained how Arthur Pinner knew of Pycroft's new job. It seems odd that a large financial house would employ a clerk without an interview.

Observations: Published originally as *The Stock-broker's Clerk*, the story takes place a few months after Watson's marriage and the events of *The Sign of Four*.

Verdict: A clever conundrum – albeit virtually identical to *The Red-Headed League* – which remains pleasantly puzzling up to the gratifyingly unexpected conclusion. 4/5

19) The Adventure of the 'Gloria Scott'

UK: *The Strand Magazine* (April 1893, SP); USA: *Harper's Weekly* (15 April 1893, WHH)

The Case: Holmes' student friend's father faces a sinister man from his shady past…

Date: Summer-autumn 1885.

Characters: Victor Trevor, Mr Trevor, Sir Edward Hoby, maid, Hudson, Beddoes, Dr Fordham, James Armitage, Jack Prendergast, Evans, Lt. Martin, Wilson.

Locations: 221B Baker Street; house in Donnithorpe, Norfolk.

Holmes: Only had one friend at college (Victor Trevor), wasn't very sociable, but did fence and box. Built his analytical system at college. Does organic chemistry in his summer holiday.

Elementary: Deduces Mr Trevor's background from his tattoo.

Quotable Quote: '(Victor Trevor) was a hearty, full-blooded fellow, full of spirit and energy, the very opposite to me in most respects; but we found we had some subjects in common, and it was a bond of union when I learnt that he was as friendless as I.'

Problems: Hudson's role and motivation go unexplained: if he is a fellow convict, why is he threatening to expose Trevor? (This would implicate him also.) If one of the crew, why does he not simply blackmail him?

Observations: Told largely in flashback by Holmes, this is his first case and one that spurred him on to make a profession of a hobby. There appears to be an equal number of clues for either Oxford or Cambridge being Holmes' college town.

Verdict: Fascinating in the light it sheds on Holmes' youth, this is nonetheless an unfocused tale that veers more towards swashbuckling piracy than crime detection. 3/5

20) The Adventure of the Musgrave Ritual

UK: *The Strand Magazine* (May 1893, SP); USA: *Harper's Weekly* (13 May 1893, WHH)

The Case: A butler and maid have disappeared, leaving behind a bag of rusty metal and a few old stones...

Characters: Reginald Musgrave, Richard Brunton, Rachel Howells, Janet Tregellis, Sir Ralph Musgrave.

Locations: 221B Baker Street; Holmes' lodgings, Montague Street; Hurlstone Manor House, West Sussex.

Recorded Cases: The Gloria Scott, A Study in Scarlet.

Unrecorded Cases: The Tarleton murders, Vamberry the wine merchant, the old Russian woman, the singular affair of the aluminium crutch, Ricoletti of the club foot and his abominable wife.

Holmes: Is very untidy – keeps his cigars in the coal scuttle, his tobacco in the toe of a Persian slipper, and his unanswered letters pinned to the mantelpiece with a knife. Shoots a 'VR' monogram in the wall with bullet holes. Keeps piles of case notes all over the place, and only files them once every year or two. Keeps a commonplace book (scrapbook). Calls Watson 'my boy'.

Quotable Quote: 'You know my methods in such cases, Watson: I put myself in the man's place, and having first gauged his intelligence, I try to imagine how I should myself have proceeded under the same circumstances.'

Problems: The sun's position relative to the earth would have changed fractionally over 300 years, leading to an inaccurate siting of the crown. And why was it twisted so violently out of shape?

Observations: Holmes' third case as a consulting detective and, like the previous story, one in which Watson hardly features, the narrative being related solely by Holmes. It appears to be inspired by Poe's short story *The Gold Bug*. An adapted version of the Musgrave Ritual was used in TS Eliot's play *Murder in the Cathedral*. The couplet 'What was the month? The sixth from the first' was omitted from the original *Strand* text but inserted into the UK version of *The Memoirs*.

Verdict: A nicely written treasure hunt with lashings of atmosphere. Holmes' intelligence and reasoning powers are never more believable. 5/5

21) The Adventure of the Reigate Squires

UK: *The Strand Magazine* (June 1893, SP); USA: *Harper's Weekly* (17 June 1893, WHH)

The Case: A murdered coachman is found clutching a fragment of a letter…

Date: 14–26 April 1887.

Characters: Colonel Hayter, Acton, Cunningham, Alec Cunningham, Inspector Forrester, *William Kirwan*, *Annie Morrison*.

Locations: 221B Baker Street; Colonel Hayter's house, near Reigate, Surrey; *Hotel Dulong, Lyons*.

Unrecorded Cases: The Netherland-Sumatra Company and the machinations of Baron Maupertuis.

Holmes: Suffers a nervous breakdown after an exhausting two-month case, leading to severe depression. A new case makes him better. Studies graphology.

Quotable Quote: '…I make a point of never having any prejudices and of following docilely wherever fact may lead me…'

Problems: It seems odd that the incriminating letter was jointly written, and then not discarded later. The burglars should have taken something of value if they had wanted to appear 'genuine'. Holmes says handwriting is hereditary – most experts say it is not.

Observations: The story was first published in the UK as *The Adventure of the Reigate Squire*. It was pluralised on its reappearance in *The Memoirs* collection in 1894. In America it is known as *The Reigate Puzzle*. It was the first Sherlock Holmes story to use a facsimile letter.

Verdict: A rather far-fetched tale concerning incompetent villains. Despite his recent illness, Holmes solves the whole thing virtually in his sleep. 3/5

22) The Adventure of the Crooked Man

UK: *The Strand Magazine* (July 1893, SP); USA: *Harper's Weekly* (8 July 1893, WHH)

The Case: A colonel is murdered, and his wife is the chief suspect...

Date: A few months after Watson's marriage.

Characters: Simpson, Teddy the mongoose, Henry Wood, Jackson, Colonel James Barclay, Nancy Barclay, Major Murphy, Miss Morrison, Jane Stewart, Coachman, General Neill.

Locations: Watson's house; the Royal Mallows barracks, Aldershot, Hants; 'Lachine', Aldershot, Hants; Hudson Street, Aldershot, Hants; *Watt Street Mission, Aldershot, Hants*; *Bhurtee, India*; *Darjeeling, India*; *Punjab, India*.

Holmes: Accuses Watson of withholding vital information in his retelling of cases. Has a working knowledge of the Bible.

Watson: His medical neighbour is Jackson.

Elementary: Deduces Watson has no guests, has had the gas fixed and has had a busy day.

Disguise: An electoral registration agent.

Problems: The morning room is facing west, so would receive little sunlight. The mongoose was carried in a box, so would not leave paw-prints.

Quotable Quote: 'Sorry to see that you've had the British workman in the house. He's a token of evil.'

Observations: Holmes comes close to uttering his immortal catchprase here ('"Excellent," I cried. "Elementary," said he'). In several editions, the name of the regiment has been changed to the Royal Munsters.

Verdict: A quirky tale that would be over far quicker were it not for Doyle's old standby of brain fever on the part of the main witness. 3/5

23) The Adventure of the Resident Patient

UK: *The Strand Magazine* (August 1893, SP); USA: *Harper's Weekly* (12 August 1893, WHH)

The Case: A wealthy patient with a heart condition fears intruders in his house…

Characters: Dr Percy Trevelyan, Inspector Lanner, *Blessington, page, Biddle, Hayward, Moffat, Sutton, Cartwright, Tobin.*

Locations: 221B Baker Street; 403 Brook Street, London.

Recorded Cases: A Study in Scarlet, The 'Gloria Scott.'

Unrecorded Case: The 1875 Worthingdon bank robbery.

Holmes: His favourite place is London and he dislikes nature (but he changes his mind on retirement – see *The Lion's Mane*).

Watson: Yearns for a holiday in the New Forest or Southsea, but hasn't enough money to go.

Elementary: Deduces Watson's train of thought on the American Civil War.

Quotable Quote: (Watson) '[Holmes] loved to lie in the very centre of five millions of people, with his filaments stretching out and running through them, responsive to every little rumour or suspicion of unsolved crime.'

Problems: In certain editions, the month is stated as October (contradicting the parliament reference), but in others it has been corrected to August. The introductory scene makes more sense where it belongs in *The Cardboard Box*, with 'close, rainy' replaced by the original 'blazing hot' (see 'Observations' below). How did the Worthingdon gang find Blessington? And why did they pose as Russians?

Observations: When this story appeared in *The Memoirs of Sherlock Holmes*, Doyle lifted the 'mind-reading' episode from *The Cardboard Box* (a tale he considered too sensational for the anthology) and inserted it here. But when John Murray published the omnibus *Sherlock Holmes: The Complete Short Stories* (1928), instead of using the original *Strand* version of this story, the 'mind-reading' was cut and replaced with two new paragraphs. Thus there are now three versions of this story: 1) The original *Strand* version; 2) the *Memoirs* version with added 'mind-reading' episode; 3) the 'new' *Complete Short Stories* version.

It is probably no coincidence that both of Watson's ideal holiday destinations are where Doyle had (or will have) homes. The ship *Norah Creina* also appears in Robert Louis Stevenson's *The Wrecker* (1891). Watson's colourful (some might say unkind) descriptions of obesity are echoed in the next story with regard to Mycroft Holmes.

Verdict: Similar in feel to *The Five Orange Pips* (revenge followed by a shipwreck), this is an intriguing little tale which has a pleasing whiff of reality about it. 4/5

24) The Adventure of the Greek Interpreter

UK: *The Strand Magazine* (September 1893, SP); USA: *Harper's*

Weekly (16 September 1893, WHH)

The Case: A Greek interpreter is coerced into interviewing a restrained and gagged man…

Characters: Mycroft Holmes, Mr Melas, Paul Kratides, landlady, Inspector Gregson, *Harold Latimer*, *Sophy Kratides*, *J Davenport*, *Wilson Kemp*.

Locations: 221B Baker Street; The Diogenes Club, Pall Mall; rooms in Pall Mall; *Wandsworth Common*; *'The Myrtles'*, *Beckenham*.

Unrecorded Case: Adams and the Manor House.

Holmes: Watson regards him as a brain without a heart. Is averse to women and doesn't usually talk about his family. His ancestors were country squires, his grandmother possibly the sister of French painter Emile Jean Vernet (1789–1863). Has consulted Mycroft many times and his brother has given him some of his most interesting cases. Has now acquired an intricate knowledge of astronomy (cf. *A Study in Scarlet*).

Mycroft: Is seven years older than Holmes, has greater observational powers than him but no energy or ambition. Founder member of the Diogenes Club, a place for people who are unsociable and unclubbable – no one is allowed to take notice of anyone else. Lodges in Pall Mall and audits books for various government departments in Whitehall. His body is corpulent but his face is almost as sharp as Holmes'. Takes snuff. Uses graphology.

Elementary: Holmes and Mycroft deduce that a passer-by is an ex-soldier, recently widowed and with two children.

Quotable Quote: 'I cannot agree with those who rank modesty among the virtues. To the logician all things should be seen exactly as they are, and to underestimate oneself is as much a departure from truth as to exaggerate one's own powers.'

Problems: Instead of going to all the trouble of renting a house and hiring an interpreter, the villains could have just faked Kratides' signature. Facial plasters are a very poor sort of disguise – why not a mask? J Davenport's role is never explained. After dragging Paul Kratides from the poisoned room, Watson doesn't bother to check if he's alive. Who sent the Budapest newspaper cutting?

Observations: The scene where the Holmes brothers deduce a man's life from his appearance was directly inspired by Dr Joseph Bell's analysis of one of his patients at Edinburgh University.

Verdict: Holmes is virtually redundant here, the actual explanation coming from Watson for a change. Once again the villains escape the law, only to receive their just deserts from another quarter. Mycroft and his club are wonderful additions to the canon. 4/5

25) The Adventure of the Naval Treaty

UK: *The Strand Magazine* (October-November 1893, SP); USA: *Harper's Weekly* (14–21 October 1893, WHH)

The Case: A top secret Anglo-Italian treaty goes missing from the Foreign Office…

Date: Late July 1889.

Characters: Percy 'Tadpole' Phelps, Lord Holdhurst, Mary Watson, page-boy, Joseph Harrison, Annie Harrison, Inspector Forbes, nurse, Mrs Hudson, *Charles Gorot, Mr and Mrs Tangey, Miss Tangey, policeman, female searcher, Dr Ferrier.*

Locations: Watson's medical practice; 221B Baker Street; 'Briarbrae', Woking, Surrey; Scotland Yard; Lord Holdhurst's chambers, Downing Street, Whitehall; *Foreign Office, Charles Street, Whitehall; 16 Ivy Lane, Brixton; Ripley village inn, Surrey.*

Recorded Cases: The Second Stain, The Speckled Band.

Unrecorded Case: The Tired Captain.

Holmes: Conducts chemical experiments to determine a man's guilt. Sits with his knees against his chin and his hands round his shins. Makes a note on his shirt cuff. Is capable of descending into a reverie about the beauty of flowers, but at other times is totally without emotion. Is an admirer of French medical statistician Alphonse Bertillon (1853–1914), who in the 1890s began studying fingerprint identification as a means of detecting criminals. Has acted for three European royal families. If he is off the scent, he admits it but when all is going well he is usually uncommunicative. Has a taste for the dramatic.

Watson: Is 'the stormy petrel of crime', according to Holmes. A petrel is a sea bird usually flying far from land. A stormy petrel is a small petrel of the North Atlantic with black and white plumage and long wings. Figuratively it means a person causing unrest (as in Watson, when he brings news of a crime to Holmes).

Quotable Quote: 'Our highest assurance of the goodness of Providence seems to me to rest in the flowers.'

Problems: It seems as if the commissionaire Mr Tangey is aware of the real culprit, but this is never followed up. Why didn't Phelps copy the treaty in shorthand? After retrieving this top-secret document, Holmes entrusts it to his landlady! (She must be *very* trustworthy.) A reference is made to the as yet unwritten *The Second Stain* which is said to feature M Dubuque and Fritz von Waldbaum. It doesn't.

Observations: This is the longest of all the short stories, the first to contain a map illustration, and also the first to be split across two issues of *The Strand*. Percy Phelps' uncle is said to be a reference to Arthur Balfour's uncle, Lord Salisbury (Robert Cecil, the Conservative prime minister and foreign secretary).

Cecil's nepotism inspired the phrase 'Bob's your uncle'. As a point of historical accuracy, between 1887 and 1896, Great Britain did have a secret treaty with Italy called the 'Mediterranean Agreements', signed by Lord Salisbury.

Verdict: The PG Wodehouse-type Phelps does a lot of ejaculating in yet another story that features sustained brain fever as a means of furthering the action. But it's an intriguing case, and one that truly exercises Holmes' deductive powers. In the charming aside about the rose, it seems that Doyle is deliberately opening up Holmes' character prior to his (intended) last appearance in print. 4/5

26) The Adventure of the Final Problem

UK: *The Strand Magazine* (December 1893, SP); USA: *McClure's Magazine* (December 1893, HCE)

The Case: Holmes is throwing his net around an evil mastermind of crime...

Date: 24 April–6 May 1891.

Characters: Professor Moriarty, Mycroft Holmes, Peter Steiler, messenger boy, *Colonel James Moriarty*, *Mary Watson*, *Inspector Patterson*.

Locations: Watson's practice, backing onto Mortimer Street; Lowther Arcade; Victoria Station; Canterbury Station; Brussels; Strasbourg hotel; Valley of the Rhône, Gemmi Pass; Englischer Hof, Meiringen; Reichenbach Falls, Switzerland; *221B Baker Street*; *Mycroft's rooms, Pall Mall*; *corner of Marylebone Lane and Bentinck Street*; *Vere Street*.

Recorded Cases: A Study in Scarlet, The Naval Treaty.

Unrecorded Cases: A French Government case in Nîmes and Narbonne, the Royal Family of Scandinavia.

Holmes: If he could beat Moriarty, he would retire – the French government alone has paid him enough to do so. Senses Moriarty's influence in a host of unrelated crimes over the years. Is casting his net over Moriarty, but needs proof to convict him – although he would risk death to bring him to justice. After 1,000 cases, he feels he would like to look into more natural mysteries. Carries a silver cigarette case.

Mycroft: Disguises himself as a coachman and is an expert at driving a cab.

Moriarty: He pervades London, but no one has heard of him. He is of good birth, clever, a skilled mathematician. At 21 he wrote a treatise on the Binomial Theorem and won a mathematical chair at a small university. But he had hereditary criminal tendencies and had to resign his post, coming to London where he set up as an army coach (presumably he 'crammed' men for the Sandhurst entrance exam). Now he controls the majority of criminals in London – they do his bidding and, if they are caught, he is never detected. Has a crime syndicate responsible for over 40 unsolved crimes. He is tall, thin, clean shaven, pale and ascetic with a domed forehead and sunken eyes. He is also round-shouldered and his head slopes forward and oscillates slightly from side to side as he talks. Has studied phrenology.

Disguise: An old Italian priest.

Quotable Quote: '[Moriarty] is the Napoleon of crime, Watson. He is the organiser of half that is evil and of nearly all that is undetected in this great city. He is a genius, a philosopher, an abstract thinker. He has a brain of the first order. He sits motionless, like a spider in the centre of its web…'

Problems: How can Holmes deduce Moriarty at work in *undiscovered* crimes? Why isn't Holmes just shot by one of Moriarty's henchmen (especially as he displays a fear of airguns)? Holmes' suggestion at Canterbury station that they change from Dover to Newhaven would have involved three changes of train and taken at least six hours – too long to arrive at Brussels the same night. Why did Moriarty not assign someone to keep an eye on the rear of Watson's house? (Colonel Moran perhaps.) Watson says a hansom cab was procured for 'us' – to whom else is he referring?

Observations: With his novel, *The White Company*, selling well, Doyle decided to kill off Sherlock Holmes to concentrate on historical fiction. While lecturing in the Swiss town of Lucerne, his travelling companion Silas K Hocking suggested the perfect place for him to despatch his creation – the famous tourist attraction of Reichenbach Falls in the Hasli Valley.

Moriarty is allegedly based on two people. Firstly, Doyle's friend Major General Alfred Drayson, a fellow member of the Portsmouth Literary and Scientific Society: he taught maths for many years and was a theoretical astronomer. Secondly Adam Harry Worth, a professional American criminal who stole a Gainsborough painting in 1876. Moriarty also bears a resemblance to a nineteenth century barrister and master forger, James Townsend Saward.

Verdict: To those who claim that Moriarty is not actually seen in this story (leading to the absurd theory that the Napoleon of crime is purely imaginary, or more absurdly, that he is Holmes himself), just look at *The Valley of Fear*, in which Inspector MacDonald actually meets him face-to-face. But silly revisionism aside, this is a fantastic grand finale – a vividly-drawn arch-villain, attempted assassinations, a desperate flight across different continents and, ultimately, a truly sacrificial death. An epic tale that rounds off the end of an era in magnificent style. 5/5

27) The Hound of the Baskervilles

UK: *The Strand Magazine* (August 1901–April 1902, SP); USA: *The Strand Magazine* (September 1901–May 1902, SP)

The Case: A legendary spectral dog has returned to kill the baronets of a desolate Dartmoor estate...

Date: Late September–October 1889.

Characters: James Mortimer, Mrs Mortimer, Inspector Lestrade, boy, John and Eliza Barrymore, Sir Henry Baskerville, Mr Frankland, Jack Stapleton, Beryl Stapleton, waiter, Wilson, Cartwright, John Clayton, spaniel, Perkins, scullery maid, postmaster, James, Laura Lyons, Anthony, the Hound, *Sir Charles Baskerville, Hugo Baskerville, Rodger Baskerville, John Baskerville, Elizabeth Baskerville, Murphy, Theophilus Johnson, Mrs Oldmore, James Desmond, Selden, Middleton, Sir John Morland, Rear-Admiral Baskerville, Sir William Baskerville, Mr and Mrs Vandeleur, Fraser.*

Locations: 221B Baker Street; Baskerville Hall, Dartmoor, Devon; Northumberland Hotel; Regent Street; Bond Street art gallery; Waterloo Station; Coombe Tracey railway station; Merripit House; Grimpen Mire; Black Tor; Laura Lyons' office, Coombe Tracey; *Bradley's Tobacconist, Oxford Street; Stanford's Map Shop; Grimpen; Lafter Hall, Fernworthy; High Tor; Foulmire; Princetown Prison; 3 Turpey Street, Borough; Shipley's Yard, near Waterloo; Trafalgar Square; Museum of the College of Surgeons, Long Down; St Oliver's private school, East Yorkshire; Ross & Mangles, Fulham Road; Mexborough Private Hotel, Craven Street; Folkestone Court.*

Unrecorded Cases: The Vatican cameos, Wilson of the district messenger office, blackmail of a well-respected person, similar incidents in Grodno, Little Russia in 1866, the Anderson murders in North Carolina, Colonel Upwood's card scandal at the Nonpareil Club, Mme Montpensier's murder charge against her daughter Mlle Carère.

Holmes: Frequently stays up all night. Has written a monograph on dating old manuscripts. Thinks getting into a box would help concentrate his mind. Can recognise many different newspaper typefaces. Has crude ideas about art. Thinks this case is the most complex of the 500 cases he has worked on. In the country he wears a tweed suit and cloth cap. Has a love of personal cleanliness. He doesn't laugh often, but when he does it means that he's closing in on his foe. Doesn't explain his plans until he's acted on them. Can differentiate between 75 different kinds of perfume. Quotes from the Bible (Matthew 6.34: 'Sufficient unto the day is the evil thereof').

Watson: Has lived with Holmes for years and is fast on his feet.

Elementary: Deduces Mortimer's career and character from his walking stick.

Quotable Quotes: 'It may be that you (Watson) are not yourself luminous; but you are a conductor of light... in noting your fallacies I was occasionally guided towards the truth.'

'In a modest way I have combated evil, but to take on the Father of Evil himself would, perhaps, be too ambitious a task.'

Problems: The arrival time of Sir Henry's train at Waterloo reduces by 25 minutes during (at most) a two-minute conversation. Holmes' false beard theory seems tenuous at best – and, if it was a false beard, then clearly it wasn't Barrymore (whose beard was real), so Watson needn't be suspicious of him. How would Holmes have heard about Laura Lyons? Even a 'cunning preparation' of phosphorescent paint can't create a flaming mouth and eyes – *can* it? Cornish tin mines are transported to Devon. What happened to Watson's missing diary page? (The story makes perfect sense without it.)

Observations: In April 1901 Doyle went on a golfing holiday to Cromer with his friend Bertram Fletcher Robinson (later editor of *Vanity Fair*). It was on this trip that Robinson regaled him with tales of spectral hounds – specifically one that haunted the Norfolk coastline called Black Shuck, and another that was said to terrorise Dartmoor.

The Dartmoor legend is as follows. In the seventeenth century Brook Manor, near Buckfastleigh on the edge of the moor, was owned by evil squire Richard Cabell (who is buried at Buckfastleigh churchyard). Cabell attacked his wife in a jealous rage, and she fled across the moor with her faithful hound. Cabell pursued and killed her, but the hound tore his throat out before dying of knife wounds inflicted by the squire. The dog was then said to appear to each new generation of the Cabell family.

Doyle had visited Dartmoor back in August 1881 but, intrigued by the tales, he and Robinson returned there less than a month after the golfing trip, both staying at Rowe's Duchy Hotel in Princetown in the shadow of Dartmoor jail. (Today the hotel is a museum.) Doyle sensed that the lonely tracts of heath and exposed moorland would make the ideal setting for a book, and they sometimes walked up to 14 miles a day exploring the area.

Doyle borrowed the topography of the moor, but changed certain names. A compound of Fox Tor Mire (where prisoners and ponies had been swallowed by oozing mud) and Grimspound Bog became the Great Grimpen Mire. The hamlet of Merripit near the prison gave its name to the fictional Merripit House. Bovey Tracey or Totnes became Coombe Tracey. The convict Selden apparently shared his name with one of Dartmoor Prison's toughest warders.

The character of Sherlock Holmes was only introduced

after the plot was decided upon, which explains his absence from much of the story. The name Baskerville was allegedly mentioned by Doyle to his mother before the Dartmoor trip, but the coachman who drove Doyle and Robinson around, Harry Baskerville, said Doyle used his name. He also claimed that Robinson had thought of the story himself and had co-written it with Doyle. This was denied by Doyle's son Adrian. (It is unclear how much input Robinson had but, in providing the central idea of the demon hound, he was probably the catalyst.)

Doyle began the novel at the Duchy Hotel, completing it on an extended journey home through Sherborne, Bath and Cheltenham to watch the cricket. For each instalment he was paid £460–£680, according to length. In the front of the book he acknowledges Robinson's help: 'This story owes its inception to my friend, Mr Fletcher Robinson, who has helped me both in the general plot and in the local details. ACD.'

Barrymore is one of the chief suspects in Sir Charles' murder, and Doyle subtly hints at this when he writes the butler was 'the first to *dog* the new heir when he returned to England' (emphasis mine). Beryl, wishing to be free of her cruel and philandering husband, is used to highlight Doyle's ongoing campaign against outmoded divorce laws.

Verdict: This is a different sort of novel to Doyle's previous efforts. There is no frantic journey, no quick succession of set pieces. Instead we have a slow, painstaking narrative with few major characters and fewer incidents. Holmes is uncharacteristically cast as an avenging man of action (that is, when he actually appears at all), while the rapport between him and Watson is strangely lacking. But the atmosphere of menace is almost tangible, and the moor itself is the book's most memorable character. The dreary final explanation, like the one in *Psycho*, should have been axed. Overall, much over-rated. 3/5

28) The Adventure of the Empty House

UK: *The Strand Magazine* (October 1903, SP), USA: *Collier's* (26 September 1903, FDS),

The Case: A familiar figure returns from his watery grave – but still in danger of his life…

Date: 30 March–April 1894.

Characters: Colonel Sebastian Moran, Mrs Hudson, Inspector Lestrade, *Ronald Adair, Hilda Adair, Edith Woodley, Mr Murray, Sir John Hardy, Godfrey Milner, Lord Balmoral, Lady Maynooth, servant, Watson's maid, Professor James Moriarty, Mycroft Holmes, Oscar Meunier, Parker, Von Herder.*

Locations: Watson's house, near Church Street, Kensington; 221B Baker Street; Cavendish Square; Manchester Street, Blandford Street; Camden House, Baker Street; *427 Park Lane, W1.*

Unrecorded Cases: Molesey Mystery, Morgan the poisoner, Merridew 'of abominable memory', Matthews 'who knocked out (Holmes') left canine in the waiting room at Charing Cross', Mrs Stewart's murder in Lauder in 1887.

Holmes: After leaving Switzerland he spent two years in Tibet, passed through Persia, then spent some months in Montpellier, France, researching coal-tar derivatives. He quotes from Shakespeare (*Antony and Cleopatra* Act 2, Scene 2: 'Age cannot wither her nor custom stale/Her infinite variety'). Wears a mouse-coloured dressing gown.

Watson: In 1904 Watson has a practice and lives in Kensington, his (first?) wife dying before 1894. Faints for the first time in his life when Holmes reappears.

Disguises: A book collector and the Norwegian explorer Sigerson.

Quotable Quote: 'Well, then, about that chasm. I had no serious difficulty in getting out of it, for the very simple reason that I never was in it.'

Problems: Why didn't Moran shoot Holmes with his airgun at some point while he was following him to the Reichenbach falls? In the original *Strand* version, the Tibetan Lama is incorrectly spelt Llama (as in the animal). Holmes could not have met the Khalifa in Khartoum because he had abandoned it in 1885 for Omdurman. Professor Moriarty bears the same Christian name as his brother in *The Final Problem*. 'Baritsu' should be 'Bartitsu,' a synthesis of Japanese self-defence methods introduced by W Barton-Wright (1860–1951) in *Pearson's Magazine* of 1899 (and therefore unknown to Holmes in 1891).

Observations: In 1903, American magazine *Collier's* made Doyle an offer he couldn't refuse – bring Sherlock Holmes back from the dead and they'd pay him more than he'd ever been paid before: $25,000 for six stories, $30,000 for eight, or $45,000 for a full thirteen. Doyle plumped for the last, and *The Empty House* was the first of the set. At *The Strand*, Greenhough Smith offered an extra £100 for every 1,000 words Doyle wrote. When released in book form as *The Return of Sherlock Holmes*, the stories were illustrated by CR Macauley.

Verdict: Not so much a mystery, more a colossal info-dump to explain Holmes' resurrection. The mannequin decoy seems naive in the extreme, and the whole tale is rather unsatisfying. 2/5

29) The Adventure of the Norwood Builder

UK: *The Strand Magazine* (November 1903, SP); USA: *Collier's*

(31 October 1903, FDS)

The Case: A solicitor is accused of killing his benefactor and burning the body...

Date: August 1894.

Characters: John Hector McFarlane, Jonas Oldacre, Inspector Lestrade, night constable, three constables, *Professor Moriarty, Verner, Mrs Lexington, Mr and Mrs McFarlane, Chief Constable, Cornelius.*

Locations: 221B Baker Street; Deep Dene House, Deep Dene Road, Lower Norwood; *Graham & McFarlane, 426 Gresham Buildings, EC; Torrington Lodge, Blackheath; Anerley Arms, Lower Norwood.*

Unrecorded Cases: The papers of ex-President Murillo (a possible reference to *Wisteria Lodge*), the Dutch steamship *Friesland*, murderer Bert Stevens in 1887.

Holmes: Dislikes publicity. When concentrating on a case, he doesn't eat, sometimes fainting from lack of energy. Thinks enough of Watson that he pays a distant relative (of Vernet?) to buy up his practice so he can move back into their Baker Street rooms.

Elementary: Deduces McFarlane's character and job from his appearance.

Quotable Quote: 'London has become a singularly uninteresting city since the death of the late lamented Professor Moriarty.'

Problems: A ruthless murderer would hardly leave such an obvious trail towards the woodpile. Bones rarely burn completely, so the remains would have pointed to an animal carcass.

Observations: The story contains the first use of fingerprints. Holmes repeats the 'false alarm' trick from *A Scandal in Bohemia*.

Verdict: A clever puzzle with a satisfying conclusion. 5/5

30) The Adventure of the Dancing Men

UK: *The Strand Magazine* (December 1903, SP); USA: *Collier's* (5 December 1903, FDS)

The Case: A Norfolk couple receives strange messages, and the wife harbours a guilty secret...

Date: July 1898.

Characters: Hilton Cubitt, Mrs Hudson, stationmaster, Inspector Martin, doctor, Saunders, Mrs King, village policeman, Abe Slaney, *Thurston, Reverend Parker, Elsie Cubitt (née Patrick), stable boy, groom, Elrige, Wilson Hargreave, Mr Patrick.*

Locations: 221B Baker Street; North Walsham railway station; *Ridling Thorpe Manor, Norfolk; Russell Square boarding house; Elrige's Farm, East Ruston, Norfolk.*

Holmes: When work is going well, he whistles and sings to himself. Is the author of a monograph in which 160 ciphers are analysed.

Watson: Keeps his cheque book locked in Holmes' drawer.

Elementary: Deduces Watson doesn't want to invest in South African securities by the chalk marks on his fingers.

Problems: Holmes could have alerted the Norfolk Constabulary by telephone the evening before the murder. Although arguably the simplest code in the canon, Holmes spends two hours deciphering it. Most versions contain mistakes in the code (in the Penguin text, for example, the 'armless man' confusingly represents both V and B). To leave a cartridge case behind, Slaney's gun must have been a semi-automatic, but they were not in common usage until after 1900.

Observations: The cipher is similar to the one Poe used in *The Gold Bug*. It is commonly thought that the Jubilee referred to is Queen Victoria's Diamond Jubilee of 1897.

Verdict: An engaging mystery that leads to a prosaic resolution. Although the client's death is striking, the tacked-on happy ending largely dispels the effect. 3/5

31) The Adventure of the Solitary Cyclist

UK: *The Strand Magazine* (January 1904, SP); USA: *Collier's* (26 December 1903, FDS)

The Case: A music teacher is shadowed by a mysterious cyclist...

Date: 23 April 1895.

Characters: Violet Smith, Bob Carruthers, Jack Woodley, Peter, *James Smith, Ralph Smith, Cyril Morton, Mrs Dixon, Miss Carruthers, Williamson.*

Locations: 221B Baker Street; Charlington Heath; Charlington Hall; Crooksbury Hill; *Chiltern Grange, Charlington, Surrey; Midland Electric Company, Coventry; Charlington Wood; Farnham police station; Morton & Kennedy, Westminster.*

Unrecorded Cases: Persecution of tobacco millionaire John Vincent Harden, the forger Archie Stamford near Surrey.

Holmes: Is prepared to defend a lady's honour with fisticuffs.

Elementary: Deduces Violet Smith is a cyclist and musician.

Quotable Quotes: '[Mr Woodley] had a fine flow of language, and his adjectives were very vigorous. He ended a string of abuse by a vicious backhander, which I failed to entirely avoid. The next few minutes were delicious.'

(Williamson) 'Put that in your pipe and smoke it, Mr Busybody Holmes!'

Problem: There seems little reason to obtain a marriage certificate when the ceremony was illegal for other reasons.

Observations: The beard disguise is reused from *The Hound of the Baskervilles. The Strand*'s Greenhough Smith objected to the fact that Holmes was not featured enough, so Doyle increased his presence.

Verdict: The premise is more interesting than the conclusion, but Holmes acquits himself like a true gentleman in defending Violet against the gang of ruffians. 3/5

32) The Adventure of the Priory School

UK: *The Strand Magazine* (February 1904, SP); USA: *Collier's* (30 January 1904, FDS)

The Case: A young boy goes missing from a northern England preparatory school…

Characters: Dr Thorneycroft Huxtable, Duke of Holdernesse, James Wilder, Heidegger, butler, peasant, Reuben Hayes, Mrs Hayes, footman, *Duchess of Holdernesse*, *Edith Appledore*, *Lord Leverstroke*, *Earl of Blackwater*, *Sir Cathcart Soames*, *Lord Saltire*, *Caunter*, *Aveling*.

Locations: 221B Baker Street; Holdernesse Hall, Hallamshire, Peak District; Priory School, near Mackleton; Ragged Shaw; Lower Gill Moor; Fighting Cock Inn.

Unrecorded Cases: Ferrers documents, Abergavenny murder.

Holmes: Is familiar with 42 different types of tyre tread. Appears to accept twice the proffered reward in return for hushing up a scandal.

Problems: The 'bicycle direction theory' is famously derided. Whichever way it was travelling, the rear wheel would always partly obliterate the track of the front one. Attempting to answer his critics, Doyle later said in *The Strand* of December 1917, 'The weight of the rider falls mostly upon the hind wheel… Thus the depth of the mark of the hind wheel would show which way the bike was travelling.' Why would a constable be patrolling a deserted crossroads in the early hours? Watson sees 'crimson' bloodstains on the gorse bush several days after Heidegger's death – but by this time, they would have lost their lurid hue.

Observations: The map illustration in *The Strand* differs slightly from the original American version.

Verdict: You wait years for a story about a cyclist, and then two come along at once! Unlike *The Solitary Cyclist* though, this is dull and goes on too long. 2/5

33) The Adventure of Black Peter

UK: *The Strand Magazine* (March 1904, SP); USA: *Collier's* (27 February 1904, FDS)

The Case: A retired whaler is found harpooned in his log cabin...

Date: July 1895.

Characters: Inspector Stanley Hopkins, James Lancaster, Hugh Pattins, Patrick Cairns, John Hopley Neligan, *Captain Peter Carey*, *Mrs Carey*, *Miss Carey*, *Slater*, *Sumner*, *Mrs Hudson.*

Locations: 221B Baker Street; Woodman's Lee, Forest Row, Sussex; *Allardyce the butcher*; *Brambletye Hotel, Forest Row*; *46 Lord Street, Brixton.*

Unrecorded Cases: The death of Cardinal Tosca (in which the Pope asked for his help), Wilson the canary trainer.

Holmes: Apart from the Priory School case, he rarely asks for a reward (like most artists, he lives for art's sake). Has five London refuges in which he can disguise himself.

Disguise: Captain Basil.

Quotable Quote: 'One should always look for a possible alternative and provide against it. It is the first rule of criminal investigation.'

Problems: The notebook would undoubtedly have been included in the inquest. Black Peter's beard sticks up after death – why? Holmes' method of handcuffing Cairns (by passing his hands over Cairns' neck) is eccentric, if not physically impossible.

Observations: At the end, it seems that Holmes and Watson are off to Norway.

Verdict: A seafaring tale that is clearly influenced by Doyle's whaling experiences as a young man, this is a pleasantly surreal story with a satisfying resolution. 5/5

34) The Adventure of Charles Augustus Milverton

UK: *The Strand Magazine* (April 1904, SP); USA: *Collier's* (26 March 1904, FDS)

The Case: A blackmailer is going about his dubious business...

Characters: Charles Augustus Milverton, secretary, Inspector Lestrade, *Lady Eva Brackwell*, *Earl of Dovercourt*, *Agatha*, *Countess d'Albert*.

Locations: 221B Baker Street; Appledore Towers, Hampstead.

Holmes: Enjoys rambling around London. Keeps a burgling kit with the latest tools. Will enter into a false marital promise if it helps solve a case. Can see in the dark. Has a hobby of opening safes. Believes certain crimes justify personal revenge, even though unlawful.

Watson: Wears rubber-soled tennis shoes. Is described as middle-sized, strongly built with a square jaw, thick neck and moustache.

Disguise: Escott, a plumber.

Quotable Quote: 'You know, Watson, I don't mind confessing to you that I have always had an idea that I would have made a highly efficient criminal.'

Problems: Milverton is a heavy sleeper and his address is public knowledge, so why has no one tried to kill him before?

(Perhaps they have, and it has been hushed up.) Holmes' unsavoury fake engagement is never resolved.

Verdict: A not entirely successful attempt to turn Holmes into a gentleman burglar like Raffles (the creation of Doyle's brother-in-law EW Hornung). There is no mystery to speak of, and the role of Holmes and Watson is marginalised. 2/5

35) The Adventure of the Six Napoleons

UK: *The Strand Magazine* (May 1904, SP); USA: *Collier's* (30 April 1904, FDS)

The Case: A madman appears to be smashing plaster busts of Napoleon...

Characters: Inspector Lestrade, Morse Hudson, Horace Harker, Beppo, Gelder & Co manager, Harding, Josiah Brown, Sandeford, *Dr Barnicot, Inspector Hill, Pietro Venucci, Lucretia Venucci, Prince of Calonna.*

Locations: 221B Baker Street; picture dealer, Kennington Road; 131 Pitt Street, Kensington; Harding Brothers, Kensington High Street; empty house, Campden House Road; Gelder & Co, Church Street, Stepney; unnamed police station; *Dr Barnicot's practice, Kennington Road; Dr Barnicot's branch surgery, Lower Brixton Road; Laburnum Lodge, Laburnum Vale, Chiswick; Lower Grove Road, Reading; Dacre Hotel, London.*

Unrecorded Cases: The dreadful business of the Abernetty family (brought to Holmes' notice by the depth to which parsley had sunk into butter on a hot day), the Conk-Singleton forgery.

Holmes: Fills a lumber-room with old newspapers. His favourite weapon is a loaded hunting crop! Enjoys attention. Is financially astute – he buys the last plaster bust at a bargain price without disclosing its real value.

Quotable Quote: (To Inspector Lestrade) 'If any little problem comes your way I shall be happy, if I can, to give you a hint or two as to its solution.'

Problems: 'Laburnum Lodge' becomes 'Laburnum Villa'. The hunt for a jewel hidden in an innocuous object is so similar to *The Blue Carbuncle* that one wonders why Holmes calls this case 'absolutely original'. Holmes gets Sandeford to sign over all rights to him, yet it is the property of neither party.

Verdict: The central concept is a clever one, and it's interesting to have a journalist actually being seen in a good light for a change. The idea of Harker being too traumatised to write the story of his own robbery is very funny. 4/5

36) The Adventure of the Three Students

UK: *The Strand Magazine* (June 1904, SP); USA: *Collier's* (24 September 1904, FDS)

The Case: A Greek examination paper has been copied before an exam...

Date: 1895.

Characters: Hilton Soames, Bannister, Daulat Ras, Gilchrist, Miles McLaren, *Sir Jabez Gilchrist.*

Locations: St Luke's College, Oxford or Cambridge.

Holmes: Is researching early English charters.

Elementary: Deduces the positions of the papers (because Soames told him).

Quotable Quote: 'Let us hear the suspicions. I will look after the proofs.'

Problems: Half a chapter of Thucydides would not fill three long slips (of foolscap?). It would be sufficient only to copy the first and last sentence of the extract, not the whole thing. Soames couldn't have got the text proofread before the next day's exams.

Observations: This story could be equally set in Cambridge or Oxford – quadrangles only exist in the latter and black clay was used for jumping pits in the former.

Verdict: A chirpy little tale with an obvious moral – cheating is *definitely* not cricket. But nice to have a simple, non-fatal puzzle that the Great Detective can solve before breakfast. 4/5

37) The Adventure of the Golden Pince-Nez

UK: *The Strand Magazine* (July 1904, SP); USA: *Collier's* (29 October 1904, FDS)

The Case: The murderer of an invalid's secretary seems to have vanished into thin air…

Date: Late November 1894.

Characters: Stanley Hopkins, Professor Coram, Mrs Marker, Susan Tarlton, Wilson, Anna, Sergius, Alexis, private detective, *Willoughby Smith*, *Mortimer*, *Chief Constable.*

Locations: 221B Baker Street; Yoxley Old Place, near Chatham, Kent; unnamed inn.

Recorded Case: The Sign of Four.

Unrecorded Cases: Crosby the banker and the red leech, contents of the Addleton barrow, Smith-Mortimer succession case, Huret the Boulevard assassin.

Holmes: Likes Alexandrian cigarettes. Has received the French Legion of Honour, which makes him a Chevalier of the Order, technically a knight. Puts women at their ease, even though he doesn't like them.

Elementary: Produces a description of the assailant from her pince-nez.

Quotable Quote: 'What did you do, Hopkins, after you had made certain that you had made certain of nothing?'

Problem: Holmes says about glasses that 'it would be difficult to name any articles which afford a finer field for inference' – the same comment he gives elsewhere in the canon about pipes, watches and bootlaces.

Verdict: The trail of clues is meticulously and fairly followed, and Holmes' analysis of the pince-nez is clever stuff. But the resolution – betrayal in a distant country – treads familiar territory. 4/5

38) The Adventure of the Missing Three-Quarter

UK: *The Strand Magazine* (August 1904, SP); USA: *Collier's* (26 November 1904, FDS)

The Case: A rugby player disappears days before a major game…

Date: February 1896/7.

Characters: Cyril Overton, hotel porter, Lord Mount-James, Dr Leslie Armstrong, coachman, Pompey the draghound, *Stanley Hopkins*, *Godfrey Staunton*, *Moorhouse*, *Morton*, *Johnson*, *Stevenson*, *Jeremy Dixon*.

Locations: 221B Baker Street; Bentley's private hotel, London; Dr Armstrong's practice, Cambridge; inn, Cambridge; *Trinity College, Cambridge*; *Scotland Yard*.

Unrecorded Cases: Arthur H Staunton the forger, Henry Staunton (whom Holmes helped to hang).

Holmes: No longer uses cocaine, but the habit is dormant within him. Thinks Armstrong could replace the void left by Moriarty's death.

Watson: Has weaned Holmes off his drug habit.

Quotable Quote: 'My ramifications stretch out into many sections of society, but never, I am happy to say, into amateur sport, which is the best and soundest thing in England.'

Problems: Holmes refers to himself as a private detective, yet earlier in *The Sign of Four* he disparaged this title, calling himself 'the only unofficial *consulting* detective'. Watson would have understood Overton's telegram, having played rugby for Blackheath (as mentioned in *The Sussex Vampire*).

Verdict: A downbeat domestic crisis, with Holmes on the periphery of the action. But as in *The Yellow Face*, he displays tact and sensitivity when faced with the personal nature of the situation. 3/5

39) The Adventure of the Abbey Grange

UK: *The Strand Magazine* (September 1904, SP); USA: *Collier's* (31 December 1904, FDS)

The Case: Robbers have apparently killed an abusive wife beater...

Date: Winter 1897.

Characters: Inspector Stanley Hopkins, Lady Brackenstall (née Mary Fraser), Sir Eustace Brackenstall, Theresa Wright, Captain Jack Croker.

Locations: 221B Baker Street; Charing Cross Station; Chislehurst Station; Abbey Grange, Marsham, Kent; Adelaide-Southampton Shipping Office, Pall Mall; Charing Cross telegraph office.

Unrecorded Case: The three Randall burglars of Lewisham.

Holmes: Thinks Watson ruins his cases by concentrating on the story rather than the science. Wants to devote his 'declining years' to a textbook on crime detection. Keeps a police whistle for emergencies. Quotes Shakespeare's *Henry V* ('The game is afoot').

Quotable Quote: 'Once or twice in my career I feel that I have done more real harm by my discovery of the criminal than ever he had done by his crime.'

Problems: Why did the assailant go to the trouble of fraying the bell rope when he had already neatly cut it? Lady Brackenstall tells Holmes that she was caught 'first by the wrist and then by the throat', but Watson mentions no bruises in either place.

Observations: Doyle obviously intended for this story to highlight the unfair divorce laws in Britain, a subject he felt strongly about. Soon after, he became president of the Divorce Law Reform Union.

Verdict: A sense of repetition is beginning to creep in here (manor house, old romance, *crime passionel*, Holmes letting the suspect go), but at least it's done with verve and style. Sir Eustace is one of the vilest creatures in the canon and commits the ultimate villainy – killing a dog. 4/5

40) The Adventure of the Second Stain

UK: *The Strand Magazine* (December 1904, SP); USA: *Collier's* (28 January 1905, FDS)

The Case: A letter that could lead to war has mysteriously vanished...

Characters: Lord Bellinger PM, Trelawney Hope, Mrs Hudson, Lady Hilda Trelawney Hope, Inspector Lestrade, PC MacPherson, Jacobs, *Oberstein, La Rothiere, Eduardo Lucas, Mrs Pringle, John Mitton, PC Barrett, Duke of Belminster, M and Mme Henri Fournaye.*

Locations: 221B Baker Street; house in Whitehall Terrace; *16 Godolphin Street, Westminster; villa, Rue Austerlitz, Paris; Charing Cross Station, London.*

Unrecorded Case: A woman at Margate.

Holmes: At the time of writing, Watson says that Holmes has retired to keep bees on the Sussex Downs.

Quotable Quote: 'Now, Watson, the fair sex is your department… the motives of women are so inscrutable.'

Problems: A tremendously important document is kept in an unguarded, unlocked room rather than a secure safe (although this was not uncommon at the time). Inspector Lestrade said he'd tidied up the crime scene – a strange practice, surely?

Observations: First mentioned in passing 11 years previously in *The Yellow Face*, this story was advertised in *Collier's* as 'The Last Sherlock Holmes Story Ever To Be Written'. Paget's illustrations imply that Bellinger was supposed to be William Gladstone.

Verdict: Despite the flawed premise, this is a pleasantly understated little tale that neatly rounds off the current series. 5/5

41) The Adventure of Wisteria Lodge

UK: *The Strand Magazine* (September-October 1908, AT); USA: *Collier's* (15 August 1908, FDS)

The Case: A guest wakes up in an empty house, his new friend and his servants having mysteriously vanished…

Date: Late March 1892.

Characters: John Scott Eccles, Mrs Hudson, Inspector Gregson, Inspector Baynes, PC Walters, *Aloysius Garcia, Melville, Lord Harringby, Sir George Ffolliott, Hynes Hynes, James Baker Williams, Henderson, Rev. Joshua Stone, PC Downing, Marx, cook, housekeeper, Lucas ('Lopez'), Miss Burnet, John Warner, Don ('Juan') Murillo, Mr and Mrs Victor Durando, José, Marquess of Montalva, Rulli.*

Locations: 221B Baker Street; Wisteria Lodge, near Esher; The Bull, Esher; *Popham House, Lee; Albemarle Mansion, Kensington; Allan Brothers, Esher; Spanish Embassy, Oxshott Common; Marx & Co, High Holborn; British Museum; High Gable, Oxshott; lodging house, Edmonton Street*; *Hotel Escurial, Madrid.*

Recorded Cases: The Red-Headed League, *The Five Orange Pips.*

Unrecorded Case: Colonel Carruthers.

Holmes: Enjoys botany.

Quotable Quote: 'My mind is like a racing engine, tearing itself to pieces because it is not connected up with the work for which it was built.'

Problems: How does Watson know Scott Eccles is the surname, and not the full name? Garcia's 1am alibi is illogical – it would still have provided enough time for him to return to Wisteria Lodge. And there is no reason for him to keep Signora Durando alive (other than that she provides the necessary solution). Did Inspector Lestrade arrive at 221B by following Scott Eccles or by (somehow) intercepting a telegram?

Observations: After *The Second Stain*, Conan Doyle wrote a set of medieval stories serialised in *The Strand* from December 1905 to December 1906, later published in book form as *Sir Nigel*. In 1906, he had a minor success with a stage production of *Brigadier Gerard* in New York. In 1907, he defended George Edalji and married Jean Leckie. He gave in and wrote two further Sherlock Holmes stories in 1908 because of public pressure and generous fees.

This story originally appeared as *A Reminiscence of Mr Sherlock Holmes* (using the spelling 'Wistaria'), spread over two issues for *The Strand*. Even taking into consideration the change of literary style over the past century, it's difficult to avoid the conclusion that Scott Eccles is homosexual. The wife of a Latin-American diplomat would be 'Señora' (Spanish) not 'Signora' (Italian).

Verdict: Another story divided into two distinct parts, but at least Holmes draws his conclusions early on, and we don't have to wait ages for the solution. Doyle has done the whole thing before much more successfully though. 3/5

42) The Adventure of the Bruce-Partington Plans

UK: *The Strand Magazine* (December 1908, AT); USA: *Collier's* (18 December 1908, FDS)

The Case: A man with stolen submarine plans is found dumped by a railway line...

Date: Late November 1895.

Characters: Maid, Mycroft Holmes, Violet Westbury, Inspector Lestrade, Colonel Valentine Walter, Sidney Johnson, railway spokesman, passenger, messenger, valet, *Arthur Cadogan West, Mason, Sir James Walter, Admiral Sinclair, Adolph Meyer, Louis La Rothière, Hugo Oberstein.*

Locations: 221B Baker Street; Woolwich Arsenal, Woolwich; Woolwich Station, Woolwich; Aldgate Underground Station; Sir James Walter's house, Woolwich; West's house, Woolwich; 13 Caulfield Gardens, Kensington; Goldini's Restaurant, Gloucester Road, Kensington; Gloucester Road Station; *Sinclair's house, Barclay Square; Woolwich Theatre, Woolwich; 13 Great George Street, Westminster; Campden Mansions, Notting Hill; Hôtel du Louvre, Paris; Charing Cross Hotel, WC2.*

Recorded Case: The Greek Interpreter.

Unrecorded Cases: Brooks, Woodhouse.

Holmes: Has begun to study the music of the Middle Ages. Has heavy tufted brows. Keeps a big map of London. Drinks curaçao (a liqueur flavoured with bitter oranges). Can totally detach himself from the case when needs be. Has written the definitive monograph on the *Polyphonic Motets of Lassus.* Receives an emerald tiepin from Queen Victoria for recovering the Bruce-Partington plans.

Mycroft: Is a man of strict habits and has only journeyed to 221B

Baker Street once before. Has a salary of £450 from a subordinate job, but is the backbone of the whole government; the knowledge of every department is passed to him, and he is consulted on every decision. Can retain a huge array of facts, neatly pigeon-holed in his brain. Is fat, and has steel-grey, deep-set eyes.

Quotable Quote: 'I play the game for the game's own sake...'

Problems: A children's party is taking place well after nine o'clock at night. Holmes was already familiar with spies (cf. *The Second Stain*, in which Oberstein receives a passing mention), so it's odd he asks Mycroft for a list. Why is the fragile Sir James in charge of such an important project? The newspaper cuttings could have been arranged in more than one way and still have made sense.

Observations: Doyle based this story on an incident that occurred to his mother's second cousin Sir Arthur Vicars, Ulster King of Arms and Chief Herald of Ireland. On 6 July 1907 the Regalia of the Grand Order of St Patrick (commonly referred to as the Irish Crown Jewels) were stolen. Although Vicars was suspected, the real culprit was allegedly Frank Shackleton, brother of Sir Ernest Shackleton the Antarctic explorer.

Verdict: Another 'stolen government document' mystery, but convincingly recounted. 5/5

43) The Adventure of the Devil's Foot

UK: *The Strand Magazine* (December 1910, GH); USA: *The Strand Magazine* (January-February 1911, GH)

The Case: Two men have gone mad and a woman lies dead in a remote Cornish cottage...

Date: March 1897.

Characters: Dr Moore Agar, Rev. Roundhay, Mortimer Tregennis, Owen Tregennis, George Tregennis, Brenda Tregennis, Mrs Porter, Dr Leon Sterndale, *Dr Richards, servant.*
Locations: Poldhu Cottage, Mounts Bay, Cornwall; Tredannick Wollas, Cornwall; *Tredannick Wartha; Beauchamp Arriance; hotel, Plymouth.*
Holmes: Dislikes fame, always preferring that the official police force gets the praise. Almost suffers a nervous breakdown due to overwork and unknown 'occasional indiscretions'. Is studying the derivation of the Celtic language.
Quotable Quote: '...if the matter is beyond humanity it is certainly beyond me.'
Problems: Holmes asks how Mortimer Tregennis heard the news – ignoring the fact that Roundhay has just told him. There seems no reason for Sterndale to carry the gravel from his cottage. Divorce laws of the time permitted a husband to get a divorce after two years of separation; Sterndale therefore could have married Brenda much sooner.
Observations: Devil's Foot is an invented poison, but could have been inspired by such plants as Devil's Bit, Devil's Guts, Devil's Fuge, Devil's Eye and Devil's Turnip. Of these, Devil's Eye (often called Henbane) is a lethal narcotic. In reality, Mounts Bay is very safe and does not attract shipwrecks.
Verdict: The surreal set-up for this story is very effective, and the scene where Watson and Holmes undergo a hallucinogenic experience is hard to forget. A fine example of Doyle imbuing the most innocent of landscapes with a palpable sense of fear and unease. 5/5

44) The Adventure of the Red Circle

UK: *The Strand Magazine* (March-April 1911, HMB & JS);
USA: *The Strand Magazine* (April-May 1911, HMB & JS)

The Case: A landlady becomes suspicious of her unseen lodger...

Characters: Mrs Warren, Inspector Gregson, Mr Leverton, Giuseppe Gorgiano, Gennaro Lucca, Emilia Lucca, *Mr Warren*, *girl*, *Tito Castalotte*, *Zamba*.

Locations: 221B Baker Street; house in Great Orme Street, Bloomsbury; high red house, Howe Street, Bloomsbury; *Morton & Waylight's, Tottenham Court Road*; *Hampstead Heath*; *Brooklyn, New York*.

Unrecorded Cases: Fairdale Hobbs (client), the Long Island Cave mystery.

Holmes: Files newspaper agony columns in a big book (the previously mentioned commonplace book?). Enjoys the music of Richard Wagner.

Quotable Quote: 'Education never ends, Watson. It is a series of lessons with the greatest for the last.'

Problems: The code! Morse would have been far quicker than the cumbersome and lengthy method chosen – and why does Holmes guess immediately that it is *not* Morse? If one flash represents 'A', two 'B' etc., then how does he know that passing the candle to and fro signifies 'vieni'? Holmes claims he flashed but the text indicates otherwise (anyway, 'vieni' would have taken at least 50 flashes). The Italian alphabet has fewer letters than the English version, so deciphering it wouldn't be as easy as Holmes suggests. Giving Emilia Lucca a false name and sending letters to her would have been easier than all this nonsense. And if Gennaro knew the Red Circle was after him, it was extremely unwise to reveal the code and source of his signals in the same newspaper advert.

Observations: The story was based on a wave of 'Black Hand' blackmail notes that plagued American immigrants before the First World War.

Verdict: Yet another American secret society after revenge. 2/5

45) The Disappearance of Lady Frances Carfax

UK: *The Strand Magazine* (December 1911, AB); USA: *The American Magazine* (December 1911, FDS)

The Case: A friendless woman has disappeared while touring Europe...

Characters: Lady Frances Carfax, Marie Devine, Moser, Jules Vibart, Dr Shlessinger, Mrs Shlessinger, landlord, Hon Philip Green, Henry ('Holy') Peters, Annie Fraser, Rose Spender, Dr Horsom, sergeant, Inspector Lestrade, *Earl of Rufton*, *Susan Dobney*, *Mrs Hudson*.

Locations: 221B Baker Street; Hôtel National, Lausanne; Englischer Hof, Baden; Scotland Yard; 36 Poultney Square, Brixton; Brixton Workhouse Infirmary; 13 Firbank Villas; Stimson & Co Undertakers, Kennington Road; *11 Rue de Trajan, Montpellier*; *Langham Hotel, London*; *Bevington's, Westminster Road*.

Unrecorded Case: Abrahams (in mortal terror of his life).

Holmes: Has a strange sense of humour. Quotes Shakespeare (*Henry VI*).

Elementary: Deduces from Watson's boots that he has had a Turkish bath.

Disguise: A French workman.

Quotable Quote: 'When you follow two separate chains of thought, Watson, you will find some point of intersection which should approximate to the truth.'

Problems: Lady Frances Carfax's family have spared no expense in employing Sherlock Holmes to find her, so they must be rather cross to learn he has sent Watson in his place. Why did it take the combined efforts of several men to prise the lid off *after* it had been unscrewed?

Verdict: One of the more original stories in this collection. Its fast pace and wide-ranging geography belie its short length, and the central idea is a good one. Holmes, though, has become somewhat thuggish. 4/5

46) The Adventure of the Dying Detective

UK: *The Strand Magazine* (December 1913, WP); USA: *Collier's* (22 November 1913, FDS)

The Case: The Great Detective is dying of a rare Asiatic disease...

Date: November 1889/90.

Characters: Mrs Hudson, Culverton Smith, Inspector Morton, Staples, *Sir Jasper Meek*, *Penrose Fisher*, *Dr Ainstree*, *Victor Savage*.

Locations: Watson's practice; 221B Baker Street; 13 Lower Burke Street; Simpson's, The Strand.

Unrecorded Case: Rotherhithe.

Holmes: He is untidy, addicted to music, indulges in pungent chemical experiments, shoots his revolver indoors, but pays handsomely for his rooms. Has considered writing a monograph on malingering.

Watson: Cannot keep secrets.

Quotable Quote: 'Shall the world, then, be overrun by oysters?'

Problems: 'Contagious by touch' is tautological. Watson's rushing off to another appointment when his friend lies dying should have raised Smith's suspicions. The bed must have been in a strange place if there was enough room for Watson's bulky form behind it, and why didn't he come out of hiding after Inspector Morton appeared?

Verdict: A great story, laced with wit and humour. Holmes seems to be enjoying his role tremendously, and even though the twist is obvious, it's undeniably satisfying. 5/5

47) The Valley of Fear

UK: *The Strand Magazine* (September 1914–May 1915, FW); USA: George H Doran (1915, AIK)

The Case: An American gold magnate is found dead in his Sussex manor house...

Date: Late 1880s.

Characters: Billy, John ('Jack') Douglas, Inspector MacDonald, White Mason, Ivy Douglas, Cecil James Barker, Ames, Mrs Allen, Sgt Wilson, Ted Baldwin, Mrs Hudson, *Fred Porlock, Professor Moriarty, Colonel Sebastian Moran, Dr Wood, Sir Charles Chandos, Jack ('Boss') McGinty, Hargrave, hotel manager, Mike Scanlan, John ('Jack') McMurdo, Jacob Shafter, Murphy, two patrolmen, Bartholomew Wilson, Jonas Pinto, bartender, Widow MacNamara, Captain Marvin, JW Windle, Andrew Rae, Treasurer Higgins, Tiger Cormac, Wilson, Foreman Blaker, Harraway, Jim Carnaway, Chester Wilcox, Archie Swindon, Morris, Fred Morris, Todman, Lee, Manson, Shuman, Van Deher, Atwood, James Stanger, Judge Lynch, Gower, Mansel, Arthur Willaby, Reilly, Evans Pott, Lawler, Andrews, Charlie Williams, Simon Bird, Jack Knox, Herman Strauss, Josiah H Dunn, Menzies, William Hales, Manders, Hunt, Evans, Mrs Larbey, Jenkins brothers, James Murdoch, Staphouse and Stendal families, Birdy Edwards, Lander, Egan, Crabbe, Carter, Steve Wilson.*

Locations: 221B Baker Street, Birlstone Manor House, Sussex; Westville Arms, Birlstone; Birlstone police station; *Hales*

Lodge, Hampstead; *Eagle Commercial hotel, Tunbridge Wells*; *Vermissa Valley, North America*; *Sheridan Street, Vermissa Valley*; *McGinty's saloon*; *Lake Saloon, Market Street, Chicago*; *Widow MacNamara's, Vermissa*; *Union House, Vermissa*; *Vermissa Herald office*; *Miller Hill, police depot*; *Hobson's Patch*; *Crow Hill*; *Stake Royal, Gilmerton*; *house at Iron Dyke crossroads.*

Holmes: Does not make friends easily. Is immune to the shock of a murder, although it does fire his intellectual capabilities – he lives for a new case. Adores genuine admiration. Enjoys toast and eggs. Is an adherent of *genius loci*, the idea that a place has a characteristic atmosphere or guardian spirit. Admits that the artist within him enjoys a well-staged performance.

Moriarty: Author of *The Dynamics of an Asteroid*, a book apparently immune to scientific criticism. Has met with Inspector MacDonald and explained how eclipses occur. Has a thin face and grey hair. Talks in a solemn, fatherly manner. Owns a painting by Jean-Baptiste Greuze (1725–1805) – a suspiciously expensive acquisition given his £700 salary. He is compared with Jonathan Wild, the eighteenth century 'thief taker' who controlled London's criminal underworld like a business venture (and was later immortalised as Mr Peachum in John Gay's *The Beggar's Opera*). His younger brother is a station-master in the west of England. Employs petty criminals to do his dirty work, with Moran his second in command (whom he pays more than the prime minister). Probably holds 20 bank accounts to disguise the extent of his ill-gotten wealth.

Quotable Quotes: (Macdonald) 'I don't take much stock of detectives in novels – chaps that do things and never let you see how they do them. That's just inspiration, not business.'

(Holmes) 'Breadth of view... is one of the essentials of our profession. The interplay of ideas and the oblique uses of knowledge are often of extraordinary interest.'

Problems: A sawn-off shotgun is very inaccurate over any great distance, so would have made a poor outdoor weapon. In the initiation ceremony, the cause (and subsequent disappearance) of the sharp points on McMurdo's eyes is never explained. Names are fluid in this story: the three Johns (Douglas, McMurdo and McGinty) are often called Jack, while McGinty is variously referred to as John, Jack, Black Jack, Boss and Bodymaster. If Holmes has successfully kept the true nature of the crime private, why then is Douglas followed to South Africa? Watson here knows of Moriarty (the impression is that Holmes has spoken many times of him), yet in the chronologically later *The Final Problem*, he's never heard of him.

Observations: William J Burns, then America's greatest detective, visited Doyle in April 1913. He spoke of his experiences of the Molly Maguires, an Irish-American secret society who terrorised the mining communities of Pennsylvania in the 1860s and 1870s. This inspired Doyle to put pen to paper on a new Sherlock Holmes novel, the first for over a decade. He changed the Molly Maguires to The Scowrers, and based the character of Birdy Edwards on James McParland, a Pinkerton operative who bravely infiltrated the organisation and brought many to justice. Boss McGinty was inspired by John Kehoe, a local Lodge president hanged in 1877 on McParland's evidence (although the detective was accused in 1905 of tampering with it).

The Valley of Fear is probably Doyle's least popular effort, mainly because of the unconnected nature of the two novellas (a criticism also levelled at *A Study in Scarlet*). German names were changed to Swedish ones prior to publication in *The Strand*. Birlstone appears to be modelled on the town of Cranbrook, Kent. 'Fortalice' is an archaic word for 'fortress' and 'acushla' is the Irish word for 'darling'. The bicycle as a means of escape is similar to *The Priory School*. Moriarty appears to have two brothers (both called James?) – one is a colonel (*The Final Problem*), and the other, mentioned here, is a station-master.

Verdict: This is an odd book (with a *huge* cast). Structurally, it is virtually identical to *A Study in Scarlet*, with the first half concerning an English murder investigation and the second detailing the bloody exploits of a religious secret society in America. But the witty and amusing Birlstone Manor section hardly prepares one for the ultra-violent second half. Indeed, the Vermissa Valley segment contains some of the nastiest and most brutal passages in the whole canon (such as a father shot down in cold blood as his five-year-old son watches). The fact that the reader is asked to empathise with a cold-blooded hitman is marginally offset by the increasingly predictable twist ending, but it's still pretty depressing stuff. The downbeat denouement, therefore, is hardly a surprise. 2/5

48) His Last Bow

UK: *The Strand Magazine* (September 1917, AG); USA: *Collier's* (22 September 1917, FDS)
The Case: A German spy secretly meets an Irish-American traitor...
Date: 2 August 1914.
Characters: Von Bork, Baron Von Herling, Altamont, chauffeur, Martha, *Jack James*, *Hollis*, *Steiner*, *Professor Moriarty*, *Colonel Sebastian Moran*, *Irene Adler*, *King of Bohemia*, *Count Von und Zu Grafenstein*.
Locations: Coast near Harwich; *Flushing, Netherlands*; *Carlton Terrace*; *Claridge's Hotel*; *Scotland Yard*.
Recorded Cases: The Empty House, A Scandal in Bohemia.

Holmes: Has been brought out of retirement from his small farm on the South Downs, where he wrote *Practical Handbook of Bee Culture, With Some Observations upon the Segregation of the Queen*. Is 60 in 1914, so was born in 1853 or 54 (unless he has aged himself as part of his disguise).

Watson: Is enlisting in his old service (presumably the Army Medical Corps).

Disguise: An Irish-American spy.

Quotable Quote:

Holmes: 'There's an east wind coming, Watson.'

Watson: 'I think not, Holmes. It is very warm.'

Holmes: 'Good old Watson! You are the one fixed point in a changing age. There's an east wind coming all the same, such a wind as never blew on England yet. It will be cold and bitter, Watson, and a good many of us may wither before its blast. But it's God's own wind none the less, and a cleaner, better, stronger land will lie in the sunshine when the storm has cleared.'

Problems: On the eve of war, why does Holmes reveal to Von Bork that his military information is faulty? (And why hadn't Von Bork already sent this information back to his German paymasters?) Carlton Terrace should be Carlton House Terrace, site of the Imperial German Embassy.

Observations: Completed on 7 March 1917, this is the first story to be written in the third person, presumably as Watson had so little involvement in the case (a fact he mentions in *The Problem of Thor Bridge*). Altamont, Holmes' alias, was Doyle's father's middle name. For the only time, Holmes is seen to travel in (though not drive) a car. Martha could well be Mrs Hudson, but this is never made obvious.

Verdict: It's good to see Holmes and Watson back in action for one last time, and they both acquit themselves wonderfully.

Doyle creates a marvellously doom-laden atmosphere and the characterisation sparkles. Considering its prime function is to stir up patriotic feelings against Germany (at the time of publication, German U-boats were a huge threat to British merchant shipping), it's a very well-written piece. 5/5

49) The Adventure of the Mazarin Stone

UK: The Strand Magazine (October 1921, AG); *USA: Hearst's International* (November 1921, FDS)

The Case: A crown jewel has been stolen...

Characters: Billy, Lord Cantlemere, Count Negretto Sylvius, Sam Merton, *Mrs Hudson, Prime Minister, Home Secretary, Straubenzee, Inspector Youghal, Tavernier, Mrs Harold, Minnie Warrender, two cabmen, Commissionaire, Ikey Sanders, Van Seddar.*

Locations: 221B Baker Street; *Scotland Yard; 136 Moorside Gardens, NW; Straubenzee's workshop, Minories; Lime Street.*

Recorded Case: The Empty House.

Unrecorded Case: Old Baron Dowson.

Holmes: Is fond of practical jokes.

Disguises: A workman and an old woman.

Quotable Quote: 'No violence, gentlemen – no violence, I beg of you! Consider the furniture!'

Problems: Holmes talks like a dime-novel Chicago gangster ('Ikey has peached, and the game is up'). A doorway could hardly be positioned within the alcove of a bay window (and there are no such windows in Baker Street anyway). It seems improbable that Holmes could have changed places with the dummy in full view of the two criminals (in the stage play the lights go out). There is only circumstantial evidence that Count Sylvius stole the jewel.

Observations: Like the previous story, this is written in the third person. It is based on Doyle's 1921 play *The Crown Diamond* (itself a retread of *The Empty House*). Colonel Moran was changed to Count Sylvius for the short story.

Verdict: This is a simplistic travesty of a Sherlock Holmes story, its roots in stage melodrama woefully obvious. 1/5

50) The Problem of Thor Bridge

UK: *The Strand Magazine* (February-March 1922, AG); USA: *Hearst's International* (February-March 1922, GPN)

The Case: A businessman's governess is blamed for his wife's death...

Characters: J Neil Gibson, Billy, Marlow Bates, Sgt Coventry, Mr Joyce Cummings, cook, Grace Dunbar, gamekeeper, doctor, villager, Ferguson, Maria Pinto.

Locations: 221B Baker Street; Thor Place, Hants.; Sgt Coventry's cottage; Thor Bridge; village inn, Hants.; *Claridge's Hotel*; *Winchester Assizes.*

Unrecorded Cases: The disappearance of James Phillimore, the disappearance of the cutter *Alicia,* the madness of Isadora Persano (caused by a worm).

Holmes: Is strongly affected by his surroundings. His professional charges are on a fixed scale (unless he foregoes payment altogether).

Watson: Keeps his papers in a tin despatch box at Cox & Co, Charing Cross. Carries a revolver on cases.

Quotable Quote: 'I do not think that in our adventures we have come across a stranger example of what perverted love can bring about.'

Problem: Isadora is not normally a man's name.

Observations: Doyle based this story on two sources: the murder of Caroline Luard on 24 August 1908 in Ightham, Kent, and a faked German suicide related by Hans Gross in his book *Criminal Investigation*.

Verdict: A brilliant story, well up to the standard of Doyle's earlier ones. 5/5

51) The Adventure of the Creeping Man

UK: *The Strand Magazine* (March 1923, HKE); USA: *Hearst's International* (March 1923, FDS)

The Case: A learned professor suddenly begins to behave strangely...

Date: 6 September 1903.

Characters: Professor Presbury, Trevor Bennett, Edith Presbury, Macphail, *Roy the wolf-hound*, *Professor Morphy*, *Alice Morphy*, *Prague student*, *A Dorak*, *Mercer*, *H Lowenstein*.

Locations: Watson's practice; 221B Baker Street; 'Chequers,' Camford; Presbury's house, Camford.

Recorded Case: The Copper Beeches.

Holmes: Observes people's hands first, then their cuffs, the knees of their trousers and finally their boots. Is considering writing a monograph on the habits of domestic dogs.

Watson: Thinks of himself as one of Holmes' many habits – a sounding board for his theories and opinions. Has a busy practice.

Quotable Quotes: 'The highest type of man may revert to the animal if he leaves the straight road of destiny.'

(Telegram) 'Come at once if convenient – if inconvenient come all the same. – SH.'

Problem: Edith refers to Trevor Bennett as 'Jack' (cf. *The Yellow Face*).

Observations: This is described as one of Holmes' last cases before retirement. A bizarre variant on Jekyll and Hyde, the story was based on Serge Voronoff's experiments in France with glandular implants from animals to men. An alienist is an archaic word for a psychiatrist. Holmes refers to himself and Watson as 'Busy Bee and Excelsior' – 'busy bee' means they are industrious, and 'excelsior' is Latin for 'ever higher'.

Verdict: More science fiction/horror than crime, and pretty eccentric with it. Far-fetched solution notwithstanding, it makes good reading even if Holmes' part is a small one. Odd to see him criticising someone for drug-taking, though, when he himself was once a user. (Perhaps he has seen the error of his ways?) 4/5

52) The Adventure of the Sussex Vampire

UK: *The Strand Magazine* (January 1924, HKE); USA: *Hearst's International* (January 1924, WTB)

The Case: A mother is seen apparently drinking the blood of her baby…

Characters: Robert ('Bob') Ferguson, Dolores, Mrs Mason, Jack Ferguson, Mrs Ferguson, baby, Carlo the spaniel, *Morrison, Morrison & Dodd, two servants, Michael.*

Locations: 221B Baker Street; Cheeseman's, Lamberley, Sussex; 'Chequers', Lamberley; *46 Old Jewry*; *Ferguson and Muirhead (tea brokers), Mincing Lane.*

Recorded Case: The 'Gloria Scott.'

Unrecorded Cases: The ship *Matilda Briggs* and the giant rat of Sumatra, Victor Lynch the forger, Vittoria the circus belle, Vanderbilt and the Yeggman, Vigor the Hammersmith wonder.

Holmes: Although he is keen to receive information, he seldom thanks people for giving it to him.

Watson: Played rugby for Blackheath.

Quotable Quote: 'This Agency stands flat-footed on the ground, and there it must remain. The world is big enough for us. No ghosts need apply.'

Problems: Doyle does not mention the name or sex of the baby. Mrs Ferguson seems willing to allow her child to die rather than explain all to her husband – a strange decision. A year at sea seems a rather weak cure for such a psychopathic juvenile – what about recruiting an alienist (cf. *The Creeping Man*)? If the information in Holmes' scrapbook about vampires was 'rubbish', why did he file it in the first place? Holmes really should have got Watson to examine the baby's wounds – it would have saved a lot of time.

Observations: This is the only story in the canon to star a villainous child.

Verdict: Just like the last story, a rather sinister premise leads to a prosaic solution – although in this case it has the benefit of a little more credibility. 4/5

53) The Adventure of the Three Garridebs

UK: *The Strand Magazine* (January 1925, HKE); USA: *Collier's* (25 October 1924, JRF)

The Case: Holmes is asked to find a man with an unusual surname…

Date: Late June 1902.

Characters: Nathan Garrideb, John Garrideb, Mrs Hudson, Howard Garrideb, Mrs Saunders, Killer Evans (*alias* James Winter/Morecroft), *Alexander Hamilton Garrideb*, *Rodger Prescott*, Inspector Lestrade, *Waldron*.

Locations: 136 Little Ryder Street, W2; Grosvenor Buildings, Aston, Birmingham; *Moorville, Kansas, USA*; *Holloway and Steele, Edgware Road*; *Rogues' Portrait Gallery, Scotland Yard*; *Brixton nursing home.*

Holmes: Has refused a knighthood for unspecified services to the Crown. Sometimes spends several days in bed. Is very distressed at the thought of Watson being injured.

Watson: Has a siesta.

Elementary: Deduces Nathan Garrideb has been in England for some time from his clothes.

Quotable Quote: 'You're not hurt, Watson? For God's sake, say that you are not hurt?'

Problems: There is enough space between the back of a cupboard and a wall for two people to hide. The phrase 'of evil memory' makes two appearances. Nathan Garrideb used to go out to Christie's or Sotheby's, which would have allowed Killer Evans to break in without such an elaborate subterfuge.

Observations: Holmes here uses the telephone for the very first time. His refusal of a knighthood contrasts with Doyle's acceptance of one in 1902 (the year of the story). Sir Hans Sloane (1660–1753) – known as 'The Great Collector' – helped found the British Museum in London. In *The Strand*, Prescott was originally named Presbury, but was changed in later versions to differentiate the character from a similarly-named one in *The Creeping Man*.

Verdict: Shades of *The Red-Headed League*, but passable enough. Holmes' obvious distress at Watson's injury is a touching moment. 4/5

54) The Adventure of the Illustrious Client

UK: *The Strand Magazine* (February-March 1925, HKE); USA: *Collier's* (8 November 1924, JRF)

The Case: A suspected murderer is due to marry a rich young woman...

Date: 3 September 1902.

Characters: Colonel Sir James Damery, Baron Adelbert Gruner, Violet de Merville, Shinwell 'Porky' Johnson, Kitty Winter, one-legged news-vendor, Sir Leslie Oakshott, Lomax, Dr Hill Barton, butler, footmen, coachman, *Professor Moriarty*, *Colonel Sebastian Moran*, *General de Merville*, *Le Brun*.

Locations: Turkish baths; Northumberland Avenue; Watson's rooms, Queen Anne Street; 221B Baker Street; Simpson's, The Strand; London Library, St James's Square; *Carlton Club*; *Splügen Pass, Austria*; *Vernon Lodge, near Kingston*; *104 Berkeley Square*; *outside the Café Royal, Regent Street*; *Glasshouse Street, W1*; *369 Half Moon Street, W1*.

Unrecorded Cases: Sir George Lewis and the Hammerford Will case, Wainwright.

Watson: Is not living with Holmes in 1902.

Quotable Quote: 'I am not often eloquent. I use my head, not my heart.'

Problems: Holmes takes his jacket into the Turkish bath. Why was he not prosecuted for burglary or at least as an accomplice to the vitriol throwing?

Observations: Holmes' single-stick skill mentioned in *A Study in Scarlet* is finally seen in practice here. Although the titular client is not revealed, clues suggest it might have been Edward VII. The happiest years of Doyle's childhood were spent at a cottage called Liberton Bank, owned by Mary Burton. Her nephew's father John Hill Burton worked in the Scottish prison service and was the inspiration for Dr Hill Barton. Holmes refers to 'my old friend' Charlie Peace, a notorious Sheffield murderer who was hanged in 1879.

Verdict: More than a hint of sex and violence punctuates this singularly sordid narrative, one in which the law can be broken with impunity providing your client is prestigious enough. 3/5

55) The Adventure of the Three Gables

UK: *The Strand Magazine* (October 1926, HKE); USA: *Liberty Magazine* (18 September 1926, FDS)

The Case: An elderly woman is offered a huge sum to sell her house and all its contents...

Characters: Steve Dixie, Mary Maberley, Susan, Mary, Inspector, Isadora Klein, footman, *Perkins, Barney Stockdale, Spencer John, Mortimer Maberley, Douglas Maberley, Sutro, Captain Ferguson, Haines-Johnson, Langdale Pike, Klein, Duke of Lomond.*

Locations: 221B Baker Street; The Three Gables, Harrow Weald; Isadora Klein's corner house, Grosvenor Square; *Scotland Yard; Holborn Bar, Holborn; Bull Ring, Birmingham.*

Quotable Quote: 'Of course, when people bury treasure nowadays they do it in the Post Office bank.'

Problems: For someone who is normally so charming to women, Holmes behaves pretty poorly to Susan. As Douglas' trunks were still on view in the hall, isn't it more likely that Haines-Johnson would have seen them and attempted to break in? Why doesn't Holmes just look in the trunks when he sees them? And why didn't he stay the night if he thought Mrs Maberley was at risk?

Observations: A house (now demolished) called 'Three Gables' existed in Biddenham, Bedford, built by Charles Edward Mallows (1864–1915). Paregoric was a tincture of opium used for the relief of pain.

Verdict: Words and phrases which today have racist overtones are unbecoming of Holmes (especially as he had shown such tolerance in the earlier *The Yellow Face*) and coupled with the weak plot, they make this one of the poorest narratives in the canon. 1/5

56) The Adventure of the Blanched Soldier

UK: *The Strand Magazine* (November 1926, HKE); USA: *Liberty* (16 October 1926, FDS)

The Case: A soldier in the Boer War has mysteriously vanished...

Date: January 1903.

Characters: James M Dodd, Colonel Emsworth, Godfrey Emsworth, Ralph, Kent, Sir James Saunders, *Mrs Emsworth*, *Ralph's wife, inspector, two constables, Baldy Simpson, Anderson, medical superintendent.*

Locations: 221B Baker Street; *Tuxbury Old Park, near Bedford, Beds.*

Unrecorded Cases: Abbey School and the Duke of Greyminster, a commission from the Sultan of Turkey.

Holmes: Thinks Watson is selfish for taking a wife.

Elementary: Deduces James Dodd fought in the Boer War.

Quotable Quote: 'It is my business to know things. That is my trade.'

Problems: Watson is married at the time of the story yet, in *The Empty House*, which is set seven years earlier, his wife is dead. (This must be a later marriage.) Why did Godfrey press his face against the glass when he only wanted to 'take a peep' at his friend?

Observations: This and the next story are the only two to be written by Holmes. Watson does not feature in either.

Verdict: Leprosy as a metaphor for the atrocities of the Boer War? Another story in which no crime takes place, although striking nonetheless for its atmosphere of horror. 4/5

57) The Adventure of the Lion's Mane

UK: *The Strand Magazine* (December 1926, HKE); USA: *Liberty* (27 November 1926, FDS)

The Case: A swimmer has apparently been scourged to death…

Date: Late July 1907.

Characters: Housekeeper, Harold Stackhurst, Fitzroy McPherson, Ian Murdoch, PC Anderson, Maude Bellamy, Tom Bellamy, William Bellamy, Sudbury, Blount, Inspector Bardle, *McPherson's dog.*

Locations: Holmes' Sussex house; cliff path, near Fulworth; The Haven, Fulworth.

Holmes: In his retirement he enjoys swimming and nature walks. Is interested in photography (he takes photographs of the victim).

Watson: Visits the retired Holmes only occasionally.

Quotable Quote: 'It has done mischief enough. Its day is over!'

Problems: At the end Holmes says he thought McPherson hadn't been in the water, yet earlier, straight after examining the body, he'd wondered why McPherson hadn't bothered drying himself (and therefore might've been in the water). As McPherson had been swimming, his body (and his hair) would have been wet, or at least smelt of salt water (Holmes exhibits an especially strong sense of smell in *The Three Gables*). He contradicts a statement he made in *A Study in Scarlet* that only a fool would clutter his brain with useless trivia – here he makes a feature of it. Why didn't he look under 'L' in one of his scrapbooks, instead of trying to remember where he'd seen the reference? Bee-keeping is not mentioned. When Murdoch appears, his students are not with him.

Observations: Writing in *The Strand Magazine* of June 1927, Doyle considered the plot of this story as 'among the best of the whole series'. Maude Bellamy's house may have been based on the Turret House, Felpham, West Sussex, once home to visionary poet and artist William Blake.

Verdict: I have no problem with the arbitrary nature of the assailant – it adds a note of realism to the text – but the characterisation of Holmes is completely off-kilter. Instead of being the possessor of a cold, machine-like intelligence as in earlier stories, he is portrayed as a simple-minded amateur. Substitute Watson's name in the narrative, though, and the story is much improved. 3/5

58) The Adventure of the Retired Colourman

UK: *The Strand Magazine* (January 1927, FW); USA: *Liberty* (18 December 1926, FDS)

The Case: A man's wife has run off with his chess-playing friend...

Date: Summer 1899.

Characters: Josiah Amberley, Rev. JC Elman, Barker, Inspector MacKinnon, *Mrs Amberley*, *Dr Ray Ernest*, *cleaner.*

Locations: 221B Baker Street; The Haven, Lewisham; The Vicarage, Mossmoor-cum-Little Purlington, near Frinton, Essex; Railway Arms, Little Purlington, Essex; *Blackheath Station, SE3.*

Unrecorded Case: Two Coptic Patriarchs.

Holmes: Using the telephone and the resources of Scotland Yard, he can get all the information he needs without leaving Baker Street. Believes chess players have scheming minds.

Quotable Quote: '...is not all life pathetic and futile?...We reach. We grasp. And what is left in our hands at the end? A shadow. Or worse than a shadow – misery.'

Problems: After finding half a sentence on the wall, Holmes says that a pencil may be found on one of the bodies. But since whoever wrote it fell unconscious, the pencil would have dropped to the floor, or still been clutched (either way, Amberley would have removed it). Barker is said to be working independently of Holmes, but then Holmes later says that he 'has done nothing save what I told him'. Who was Holmes' agent? The message 'We we' is hardly proof of murder. Opening a few windows would have allowed the gas to disperse without recourse to hiding it with paint smells.

Observations: Doyle introduces a rival sleuth in this story, the only one in which the villain comes to Holmes for help.

Verdict: The actual plot may be mundane, but one senses that Doyle, with the experience of age, is at last mirroring the world in which he lives – crime *is* largely mundane. It would have been fascinating if Doyle had introduced Barker two decades earlier so we could have seen the two amateur detectives slugging it out. 4/5

59) The Adventure of the Veiled Lodger

UK: *The Strand Magazine* (February 1927, FW); USA: *Liberty* (22 January 1927, FDS)

The Case: A former circus performer tells Holmes about an old crime...

Date: Late 1896.

Characters: Mrs Merrilow, Eugenia Ronder, *Ronder, Sahara King the lion, Leonardo, Jimmy Griggs, Inspector Edmunds.*

Locations: 221B Baker Street; Mrs Merrilow's house, South Brixton; *Abbas Parva, Berks.*

Unrecorded Case: The politician, the lighthouse and the trained cormorant.

Holmes: Was in active practice for 23 years, 17 of which were spent with Watson.

Quotable Quote: 'The example of patient suffering is in itself the most precious of all lessons to an impatient world.'

Problems: Watson's 17 years with Holmes began in 1881 and ended in 1903. Adding the three-year 'hiatus' after Reichenbach, this still leaves two years unaccounted. Why did Eugenia not contact Holmes herself? She is said to be 'wasting away', yet her figure is 'full and voluptuous'.

Observations: Holmes' detective skills go unused in this flash-back narrative.

Verdict: Intriguing only as a footnote to a previously un-recorded case, this story could hardly be termed an 'adventure'. 3/5

60) The Adventure of Shoscombe Old Place

UK: *The Strand Magazine* (April 1927, FW); USA: *Liberty* (5 March 1927, FDS)

The Case: A racehorse owner is seen digging up an old body…

Characters: Sir Robert Norberton, John Mason, page, spaniel, Josiah Barnes, Mr and Mrs Norlett, *Inspector Merivale, Sam Brewer, Lady Beatrice Falder, Sir James Norberton, Shoscombe Prince (horse), Barnes, Stephens, Carrie Evans, Sandy Bain, Harvey, Sir William Falder, Sir Denis Falder.*

Locations: 221B Baker Street; Shoscombe Old Place, Berks.; 'Green Dragon,' Crendall, Berks.; Shoscombe railway station; chapel, Shoscombe Park.

Unrecorded Cases: St Pancras and the picture-frame maker, a coiner.

Watson: Uses half his invalid pension to bet on horse racing.

Quotable Quote: (Famous Last Words) 'It is nearly midnight,

Watson, and I think we may make our way back to our humble abode.'

Problem: Holmes discovers they had forgotten their bait, but then later catches enough trout for dinner.

Verdict: Despite the references to Jewish moneylenders, which nowadays strike a jarring note, the story itself is intriguing as a darker version of *Silver Blaze*. But in a perfect world you'd expect Doyle's last Sherlock Holmes story to be more dramatic than this rather limp offering, which doesn't even feature a serious crime. 3/5

The Canon in Book Form

A Study in Scarlet (first novel, 1888 [USA 1890])

The Sign of Four (second novel, 1890 [USA 1891])

The Adventures of Sherlock Holmes (first collection, 1892)
Containing: *A Scandal in Bohemia, The Red-Headed League, A Case of Identity, The Boscombe Valley Mystery, The Five Orange Pips, The Man with the Twisted Lip, The Blue Carbuncle, The Speckled Band, The Engineer's Thumb, The Noble Bachelor, The Beryl Coronet, The Copper Beeches*

The Memoirs of Sherlock Holmes (second collection, 1894)
Containing: *Silver Blaze, The Yellow Face, The Stockbroker's Clerk, The 'Gloria Scott', The Musgrave Ritual, The Reigate Squires, The Crooked Man, The Resident Patient, The Greek Interpreter, The Naval Treaty, The Final Problem*

The Hound of the Baskervilles (third novel, 1902)

The Return of Sherlock Holmes (third collection, 1905) Containing: *The Empty House, The Norwood Builder, The Dancing Men, The Solitary Cyclist, The Priory School, Black Peter, Charles Augustus Milverton, The Six Napoleons, The Three Students, The Golden Pince-Nez, The Missing Three-Quarter, The Abbey Grange, The Second Stain*

The Valley of Fear (fourth novel, 1915)

His Last Bow (fourth collection, 1917) Containing: *Wisteria Lodge, The Cardboard Box, The Red Circle, The Bruce-Partington Plans, The Dying Detective, The Disappearance of Lady Frances Carfax, The Devil's Foot, His Last Bow*

The Case-Book of Sherlock Holmes (fifth collection, 1927) Containing: *The Illustrious Client, The Blanched Soldier, The Mazarin Stone, The Three Gables, The Sussex Vampire, The Three Garridebs, The Problem of Thor Bridge, The Creeping Man, The Lion's Mane, The Veiled Lodger, Shoscombe Old Place, The Retired Colourman*

Literary Pastiches and Parodies

A good way to measure the appeal of any fictional character is to see how many imitations it spawns. Using this criterion, Sherlock Holmes is *very* popular.

The first theatrical parody of the detective was Charles H E Brookfield and Seymour Hicks' *Under the Clock, or 'Sheerluck'*, which opened at London's Royal Court Theatre on 25 November 1893, followed some years later by Malcolm Watson and Edward La Serre's more well-known *Sheerluck Jones* or *Why D'Gillette Him Off?*, a 1901 music-hall burlesque on William Gillette's 1899 stage play. There have been plenty of sketches, burlesques and short films spoofing Holmes since then but, given the limited space, it would be wiser to forgo these often meretricious offerings and concentrate, however briefly, on a far more interesting phenomenon: the literary pastiche.

According to Microsoft's Encarta World Dictionary, a pastiche is defined as 'a piece of creative work, for example, in literature, drama or art, that imitates and often satirises another work or style'. Well, there are the occasional bites of satire, but mostly these new adventures are content to rekindle the homely nineteenth century atmosphere of swirling fog, gaslit cobbled streets and abstruse murder mysteries in sprawling country houses that Doyle described so well.

The division between parody and pastiche is a fine one, and most of this section concerns the latter. Having said that, the first recorded parody was by *Peter Pan* author JM Barrie in 1893. A collaborator with Doyle on the failed opera *Jane Annie*, he presented his fellow author with *The Adventure of the Two Collaborators*, a short spoof written inside a gift book. Many parodies followed, in such publications as *Punch* and *The Bohemian*, with Doyle himself contributing one in the form of *The Field Bazaar*, a fund-raiser that appeared in the Edinburgh University magazine *The Student* of 20 November 1896.

Hundreds of parodies appeared between 1896 and 1920 – including 97 adventures of 'Herlock Sholmes' and 'Dr Jotson' by Charles Hamilton – but it was arguably Vincent Starrett's privately published 1920 short story *The Adventure of the Unique Hamlet* (republished in 1940) that inspired writers the world over to imitate the style of Sir Arthur Conan Doyle. After Doyle's death, a short story called *The Man Who Was Wanted* (aka *The Adventure of the Sheffield Banker*) was discovered amongst his papers; this turned out to be a clever pastiche written by Arthur Whitaker who had sold the story to Doyle for ten guineas.

Holmes appeared in six of Maurice Leblanc's Arsène Lupin books, beginning with the short story *Herlock Sholmes Arrives Too Late* (the name cunningly altered for legal reasons) in his 1905 collection *Arsène Lupin, Gentleman Cambrioleur*. He is last mentioned five years later in Leblanc's epic *813* (1910).

Doyle's son Adrian, a vigorous defender of his father's integrity, wrote six pastiches himself (and six with crime novelist John Dickson Carr) for *The Exploits of Sherlock Holmes* in 1954. Other short stories that appeared around this time can be found in *The Further Adventures of Sherlock Holmes*, edited by Richard Lancelyn Green.

The first new Holmes novel appeared in 1966: *A Study in Terror* by Paul W Fairman was based on the film of the same name, with a contribution by 'Ellery Queen' (Fred Dannay and Manfred B Lee). The book had Holmes pursuing Jack the Ripper, an idea echoed in later years by Michael Dibdin in *The Last Sherlock Holmes Story* (1978), John Hopkins in *Murder by Decree* (1979) and Edward B Hanna in *The Whitechapel Horrors* (1996).

But it was Nicholas Meyer's *The Seven-Per-Cent Solution* (1974) that marked the first real commercial success for a pastiche. Here Holmes met a real-life celebrity (in this case, Sigmund Freud) and set a trend for many future tales. Theodore Roosevelt appeared in H Paul Jeffers' *The Adventure of the Stalwart Companions* (1978), Bertrand Russell in Randall Collins' *The Case of the Philosopher's Ring* (1978), Houdini in Lee Matthias' *The Pandora Plague* (1981) and HP Lovecraft in *Pulptime* (1984) by PH Cannon.

No less successful have been meetings with fictitious characters. Thus we find Dr Jekyll in Loren Estleman's *Dr Jekyll and Mr Holmes* (1979), the Phantom of the Opera in Nicholas Meyer's *The Canary Trainer* (1994), Dr Fu Manchu in Cay Van Ash's *Ten Years Beyond Baker Street* (1984) and Tarzan in Philip José Farmer's *The Adventure of the Peerless Peer* (1974).

Several authors have chosen to set the detective against the Prince of the Undead. Estleman began the ball rolling in 1978 with *Sherlock Holmes vs Dracula*, the same year that Fred Saberhagen gave us *The Holmes-Dracula File*. Later additions include *The Tangled Skein* (1992) by David Stuart Davies and *Anno Dracula* (1993) by horror writer Kim Newman.

Science fiction authors have had a field day with Doyle's characters. In *Exit Sherlock Holmes* (1977) by Robert Lee Hall, Holmes and Watson are revealed to be visitors from the future. And in Andy Lane's excellent pastiche *Doctor Who: All-Consuming Fire* (1994) the Doctor from Gallifrey meets the Doctor (and Detective) from Baker Street in a stirring tale of alien monsters and spontaneous human combustion. Anthologies on the subject include *Sherlock Holmes Through Time and Space* (1984) edited by Isaac Asimov, Martin Harry Greenberg & Charles G Waugh, and *Sherlock Holmes in Orbit* (1995) edited by Greenberg and Mike Resnick.

Holmes' analytical approach has been put to good use in several thinly-disguised teaching manuals too. Thus we have *The Chess Mysteries of Sherlock Holmes* (1980) by Raymond Smullyan, *Sherlock Holmes, Bridge Detective* (1973) by Frank Thomas and, perhaps most bizarrely, *Elementary BASIC and Elementary PASCAL* (1982) by Henry Ledgard and Andrew Singer.

A popular conceit, as with the Jack the Ripper books, is to allow Holmes to clear up true-life mysteries. Val Andrews (probably the most prolific living writer of Sherlockian pastiche) persuaded us that the Great Detective solved the murder of stage magician Chung Ling Soo in *Sherlock Holmes and the Wood Green Empire Mystery* (1985). A solution to the disappearance of the Mary Celeste is postulated in Sam Benady's *Sherlock Holmes in Gibraltar* (1990) and, in *The Truth About Ludwig II* (1978), German author Zeus Weinstein presents a convincing reason for the demise of the mad king of Bavaria.

There will always be some who insist that Watson and Holmes were lovers, and Rohase Piercy's *My Dearest Holmes* (1988) is at least mercifully tasteful about the subject. The same cannot be said about 1993's *The Sexual Adventures of Sherlock Holmes* by Larry Townsend. The same year also saw Sena Jeter Naslund trying to convince us that Holmes fell in love with his own half-sister in *Sherlock in Love*. True

Sherlockians would have none of it.

Another twist of literary pastiche is to focus on someone other than Holmes. For example, the Baker Street Irregulars (the street urchins, not the august society) are the stars of Robert Newman's 1978 book *A Puzzle for Sherlock Holmes*; they also crop up in Porter Jones' *The Quallsford Inheritance* (1986) and *The Glendower Conspiracy* (1990). A more adventurous Mycroft takes the lead in *Enter the Lion* (1979) by Michael P Hodel and Sean M Wright, while Glen Petrie featured him in a short series of books starting with *The Dorking Gap Affair* in 1989.

Inspector Lestrade is probably the most obvious candidate for elaboration. He is the star of a series of fourteen wicked parodies by MJ Trow, beginning with *The Adventures of Inspector Lestrade* in 1985. In a clever reversal to the normal way of things, Holmes and Watson are frauds while Inspector Lestrade emerges as the hero. As to the female characters, Mrs Hudson takes on the detective's role in Sidney Hosier's *Elementary, Mrs Hudson* (1996) and Irene Adler makes her own way in a man's world in *Good Night, Mr Holmes* (1990) by Carole Nelson Douglas.

Moriarty as hero may be an unlikely premise, but it's exploited to the hilt in Michael Kurland's *The Infernal Device* (1978). A sequel, *Death by Gaslight*, appeared four years later. Thankfully, John Gardner's *The Return of Moriarty* (1974) and Austin Mitchelson and Nicholas Utechin's *The Earthquake Machine* (1976) both resurrect him as the blackguard that he is.

The Beekeeper's Apprentice (1994) was the first in an intriguing series by Laurie R King that had inquisitive teenager Mary Russell meeting a retired Holmes during the First World War. The couple join forces to solve various crimes, including the reappearance of a gigantic hound in *The Moor* (1998). By *The*

Game (2004), they have set aside the enormous age difference and become husband and wife.

Books influenced by Holmes, but not directly featuring him, are also popular. The hero of Julian Symons' 1975 novel *A Three Pipe Problem* is Sheridan Haynes, a Sherlock Holmes thespian who assumes the characteristics of his alter ego to solve a murder case. Then there are the entertaining books by Terrance Dicks about a group of London schoolchildren who adopt the detective's methods to investigate local mysteries; the series began with *The Case of the Missing Masterpiece* in 1978. *The Sherlock Effect* (1997) by Raymond Kay Lyon has Christopher Sherlock Webster following in the footsteps of his (middle) namesake by setting up a detective agency in Baker Street.

And one mustn't forget August Derleth's Solar Pons stories, published in book form from 1945 onwards. Pons is an Edwardian detective who impersonates Holmes, and the charm rests in the fact that he and the reader are fully aware of this. (After Derleth's death in 1971, the British author Basil Copper continued Pons' adventures with a further 12 books.) He is a character in his own right, although clearly influenced by the Baker Street detective.

Some other pastiche writers of note are LB Greenwood, Barrie Roberts and Richard L. Boyer, whose novel *The Giant Rat of Sumatra* (1976) is considered by some to be one of the best ever written. Among the more recent short story writers are Denis O Smith (still writing) and June Thompson, whose first collection, *The Secret Files of Sherlock Holmes*, appeared in 1990. A year later, the Dickens/Doyle crossover, *The Disappearance of Edwin Drood* (1991), was concocted by author and historian Peter Rowland.

More recent notable pastiches include Jamyang Norbu's *The*

Mandala of Sherlock Holmes (2001), which describes in loving detail the detective's adventures in Tibet during 'the great hiatus', and David Stuart Davis' *The Veiled Detective* (2004), which adds a fascinating new slant to the seemingly intractable characters.

It has often been said that any true Sherlock Holmes fan will have attempted a pastiche or two in their lifetime. If that is so, this short essay represents just a wafer-thin scraping of ice from the tip of a massive iceberg. The one thing we can all be sure of is that, as we head boldly into the third millennium, the Great Detective will always be there.

An A-Z of Sherlock Holmes Actors

Since 1893 Doyle's Sherlock Holmes stories have been adapted for theatre, cinema, radio and television. Many hundreds of actors have assumed the role of Holmes in a bewildering variety of original adaptations, pastiches and spoofs. Some have proven successful, others not, but each actor has added his own distinctive interpretation to the famous character, and each new production provides a fascinating record of how the Great Detective and his stories are perceived. So here, for the first time, is an alphabetical checklist of over 180 actors who've shaped the character of Holmes in the public consciousness. As a general rule I have only featured English-speaking actors (except in the case of silent films in which nationality is unimportant), and have attempted to make it as exhaustive as possible. I apologise in advance if your favourite Holmes is missing, but I hope the overall comprehensiveness of the list outweighs any minor omissions.

Note: Foreign film titles have been translated. Solely non-UK performances have been excluded, as have UK provincial productions (barring a few exceptional cases), burlesques, music-hall sketches and revues. A name in **bold** indicates a separate entry.

Hans Albers – One of the leading German actors of his time, he starred in *The Man Who Was Sherlock Holmes* (1937, UFA), a bizarre comedy in which Holmes and Watson meet their creator Arthur Conan Doyle.

Joacquim de Almeida – Portuguese actor who starred as Holmes in the 2001 Brazilian/Portuguese co-production *The Xango from Baker Street*, detailing the theft of a Stradivarius violin in Rio de Janeiro.

Georg Årlin – Swedish actor who starred in *The Three Students* (27 December 1959) and *The Golden Pince-Nez* (3 January 1960) for Swedish Channel 1 television. A decade later, *The Hound of the Baskervilles* was shown on the same channel from 9 January to 6 February 1971.

Felix Aylmer – Distinguished British stage actor who appeared in the play *The Holmeses of Baker Street* by Basil Mitchell (in which Holmes is seen to have a daughter). It was first performed at the Lyceum Theatre, Edinburgh, on 23 January 1933 followed by several months' touring.

Tom Baker – Extrovert former *Doctor Who*, miscast as Holmes in a four-part BBC production of *The Hound of the Baskervilles* produced by Barry Letts. It was shown on 3–24 October 1982. Baker later appeared in the stage play *The Mask of Moriarty* (October 1985) at the Gate Theatre, Dublin, for 51 performances (playing Holmes *and* Moriarty).

Alec Baldwin – Hollywood actor who starred in Steve Lawson's adaptation of *A Study in Scarlet* presented at the Williamstown Theatre Festival, Williamstown, Massachusetts from 12–23 August 1987.

John Barrymore – Philadelphia-born charismatic 1920s matinée idol who eventually abused his talent through alcoholism and became too unreliable to employ. Dubbed the 'Great Profile', he was launched as Sherlock Holmes by Sam

Goldwyn in 1922 in another film version of **William Gillette**'s stage play, *Sherlock Holmes*. It was called *Moriarty* in the UK, to avoid clashing with the popular Stoll series starring **Eille Norwood**.

St John Beecher – Toured the UK provinces with *The Bank of England* from 1900 (see **John F Preston**).

Harry Benham – American actor who played the title role in Thanhouser's 1913 film *Sherlock Holmes Solves The Sign of Four* (UK: *The Sign of Four*).

Grendon Bentley – Appeared in the UK provincial tour of Doyle's play *The Speckled Band* from September 1910.

Carlyle Blackwell – Busy American matinee star of the 1910s and 1920s, Blackwell had the privilege of starring in the last silent Sherlock Holmes film, 1929's *The Hound of the Baskervilles* (Erda-Film-Productions GmbH). Made in Berlin, the production featured an eclectic cast of German, Italian, Russian, English and American actors. It was scripted by Richard Oswald, responsible for the first *Hound* film adaptation in 1914 (see **Alwin Neuss**).

Michael Blagdon – Played a young Holmes in flashback scenes in *The Seven-Per-Cent Solution* (see **Nicol Williamson**).

John Blake – Appeared in the Birmingham Repertory Company's production of **William Gillette**'s play *Sherlock Holmes* at the Alexandra Theatre, Birmingham, from June 1926.

Sydney Bland – Starred in the UK provincial tour of Doyle's play *The Speckled Band* from July 1910.

Ernest Bliss – Appeared on the UK tour of **William Gillette**'s play *Sherlock Holmes* from 26 December 1901.

Jan Blomberg – Starred in a four-part *Sherlock Holmes* series for Swedish Channel 3 (17 February to 10 March 1974).

Ferdinand Bonn – German actor who first appeared in two

Berlin stage productions, *Sherlock Holmes* (1906) and *The Hound of the Baskervilles* (1907), before appearing in the 1914 Vitascope film *Sherlock Holmes Against Dr Mors*. Four years later he starred in a series for the German company Kowo GmbH (following on from **Hugo Flink**). The titles were *What He Saw in the Mirror*, *The Poisoned Seal*, *The Fate of Renate Yongk* and *The Cardinal's Snuffbox*.

Herbert Bradford – Appeared in the UK provincial tour of Doyle's play *The Speckled Band* from July 1910.

James Bragington – In 1914, Birmingham filmmaker GB Samuelson was casting around for a suitable Holmes for his adaptation of *A Study in Scarlet*. He eventually settled on an accountant at his Birmingham office for the simple reason that he physically resembled the part. (In the silent film era, looks were everything.) A glass studio was built at Worton Hall, Isleworth, and location filming – a rare luxury – took place at Cheddar Gorge (representing the Rockies) and Southport beach (the Salt Lake plains). Released in December 1914, this first British adaptation of a Sherlock Holmes story garnered rave reviews, and led to another first for Samuelson in 1916 – the first film version of *The Valley of Fear* (see **HA Saintsbury**).

Kurt Brenkendorff – German actor chosen to make one further film for Kowo GmbH, Germany, after **Ferdinand Bonn** finished in the role. Made in 1919, it was entitled *Murder in the Hotel Splendid*.

Jeremy Brett – Good-looking leading man who starred in a major series for Granada TV under the supervision of Michael Cox and then June Wyndham Davies. David Burke was Watson for the first two series, followed by Edward Hardwicke for the others. The series were as follows: *The Adventures of Sherlock Holmes* (24 April–5 June 1984), *The*

Adventures of Sherlock Holmes (25 August–29 September 1985), *The Return of Sherlock Holmes* (9 July–20 August 1986), *The Sign of Four* (29 November 1987), *The Return of Sherlock Holmes* (6–27 April 1988), *The Hound of the Baskervilles* (31 August 1988), *The Case-Book of Sherlock Holmes* (21 February–28 March 1991), *The Master Blackmailer* (2 January 1992), *The Four Oaks Mystery* (18 July 1992 as part of ITV's telethon appeal), *The Last Vampyre* (27 January 1993), *The Eligible Bachelor* (3 February 1993) and *The Memoirs of Sherlock Holmes* (7 March–11 May 1994).

Brett also starred with Hardwicke in the stage play *The Secret of Sherlock Holmes* by Jeremy Paul. It opened at the Yvonne Arnaud Theatre, Guildford, Surrey, on 30 August 1988 (as *A Case for Sherlock Holmes*), then transferred to the Richmond Theatre, Surrey, on 12 September. Its London run at the Wyndham's Theatre began on 22 September 1988 and continued until 16 September 1989. It then toured 11 venues, finishing at the Theatre Royal, Bath, on 16 December 1989. Brett died of heart failure on 12 September 1995. For many, he is the definitive Sherlock Holmes.

Clive Brook – Handsome British leading man who appeared in, and co-directed, *The Return of Sherlock Holmes* (Paramount, 1929), notable as the first Holmes film with a soundtrack (although a silent version was also released). Set on board a cruise liner, the story shows Holmes disguising himself as an orchestra violinist to help locate the boyfriend of Watson's daughter. The climax sees Moriarty attempting to kill Holmes with a poisoned thorn. Brook sent up the role in *Murder Will Out*, a sketch in the 1930 film revue *Paramount on Parade*. His second appearance was in *Sherlock Holmes*, made by Fox in 1932 (a 'terrible film', he said afterwards). Replacing Watson with page-boy Billy, director William K Howard turned in a polished and fast-paced production, albeit jarringly Americanised. The script was by Bertram Millhauser, who would later work on the **Basil Rathbone** series for Universal.

CHE Brookfield – The first actor to play Holmes on stage, in *Under the Clock* (1893), 'an extravaganza in one act', co-written by Brookfield and Seymour Hicks (who also played Watson).

Laidman Browne – Featured in *Silver Blaze*, part of the *Corner in Crime* series for the BBC radio's Home Service on 17 May 1945.

Charles Buckmaster – Toured in the 1927 UK production of *The Return of Sherlock Holmes* (see **Eille Norwood**).

Eugen Burg – German actor who appeared in Projections AG Union's *The Dark Castle* (1915), a direct rival to the same year's *The Uncanny Room*, and both subtitled *The Hound of the Baskervilles III*. (See **Alwin Neuss**.)

Alfred Burke – Appeared in **William Gillette**'s stage play at the Birmingham Repertory Theatre in March 1952.

Richard Butler – Starred in John Arthur Fraser's play *Sherlock Holmes, Detective* at the Hopkins' Theater, Chicago, from 5 May 1901.

Michael Caine – Prolific cockney leading man who played Holmes as a drunken actor in director Thom Eberhardt's fairly amusing comedy film *Without a Clue* (Rank/ITC, 1988).

Simon Callow – Played Holmes in *The Seven-Per-Cent Solution*, dramatised by Denny Martin Flinn and broadcast on BBC Radio 4 on 9 January 1993, with Ian Hogg as Watson. Six more original stories aired on BBC Radio 5 from 14 February to 28 March 1993, with Watson played by Nicky Henson.

Laurence Carter – Appeared on Leo Trood's UK tour of **William Gillette**'s play *Sherlock Holmes* from February 1919.

Michael Cashman – Former *Eastenders* actor who starred in a UK touring production *The Return of Sherlock Holmes* by Ernest Dudley in 1997.

Hubert S Chambers – Toured the UK provinces with *The Bank of England* from 1900 (see **John F Preston**).

John Cheatle – Played Holmes in a BBC Home Service biography of John H Watson, July 1943.

John Cleese – *Monty Python* star who appeared in an 'authorised' spoof called *Elementary, My Dear Watson* on 18 January 1973, as part of the *Comedy Playhouse* series for BBC TV. Four years later he again sent up Holmes in the dire *The Strange Case of the End of Civilisation As We Know It* for LWT. His and Arthur Lowe's talents were thrown to the wind by the appalling script, jointly written by Cleese.

H Cooper Cliffe – Starred in the 1914 American touring production of Doyle's play *The Speckled Band*.

Tom Conway – British light leading actor who took over from **Basil Rathbone** in the American radio series. *The New Adventures of Sherlock Holmes* was broadcast on WJZ-ABC from 12 October 1946 to 7 July 1947 (39 stories). Nigel Bruce continued as Watson.

Peter Cook – British humorist who played Holmes in an embarrassingly awful 1977 film spoof of *The Hound of the Baskervilles* (Hemdale/Michael White). His comedy partner Dudley Moore was Watson.

Harry H Corbett – Comedy actor who played the delusional Justin Playfair in James Goldman's stage play *They Might Be Giants* (Theatre Royal, Stratford, from 28 June 1961), filmed ten years later with **George C Scott**.

Maurice Costello – A well-known American stage actor, later to become a cinema matinée idol. His claim to fame is that he is the first (named) actor to have played Holmes. (A 49-second 1900 film called *Sherlock Holmes Baffled* was Holmes' first celluloid excursion, but the actor playing him is unknown.) Costello's attempt, *The Adventures of Sherlock Holmes* (also known in the UK as *Sherlock Holmes* or *Held to Ransom*) ran for 12 minutes and was loosely based on *The Sign of Four*. It was produced by the Vitagraph Company in 1903 and directed by Sheffield-born film pioneer J Stuart Blackton.

JS Crawley – Appeared on the UK tour of **William Gillette**'s play *Sherlock Holmes* from 26 December 1901.

Benedict Cumberbatch – Played Holmes in Mark Gatiss and Steven Moffat's television series *Sherlock* (2010-present). Set in the twenty-first century, these modernised tales were broadcast on BBC1 and featured Martin Freeman as Watson and Andrew Scott as Moriarty. As of writing, six stories have aired. *A Study in Pink*, *A Scandal in Belgravia*, *The Hounds of Baskerville* and *The Reichenbach Falls* were loose adaptations of Conan Doyle's original tales.

Peter Cushing – Chisel-featured star of British horror films, his first outing as the Great Detective took place in 1959 for the seventh cinematic version of *The Hound of the Baskervilles*, a Hammer production directed by Terence Fisher. Curiously bloodless (despite the fact that this was the first Sherlock Holmes film to be made in colour), the film was not a success. Cushing returned to the role in 1968, drafted in to replace **Douglas Wilmer** for a third series of 16 adaptations for BBC television. It played up the sex and savagery of the stories, but the less-than-satisfactory performance from Cushing, combined with generally amateur production values, lessened the impact. Many years later, at the age of 71, he played a retired Holmes in *The Masks of Death* (1984), a Tyburn production for Channel 4.

Henry S Dacre – Replaced **John Webb** in the 1894 stage play *Sherlock Holmes* by Charles Rogers, later appearing on the

UK tour of **William Gillette**'s *Sherlock Holmes* from 26 December 1901.

James D'Arcy – Charismatic young British actor who played Holmes to Roger Morlidge's Watson in the dire American TV movie *Sherlock* (aka *A Case of Evil*), also featuring Vincent D'Onofrio as Moriarty.

Hamilton Deane – Appeared in his own company's UK tour of **William Gillette**'s play *Sherlock Holmes* from 1923.

Robert Downey Jr. – First appeared as Holmes in Guy Ritchie's 2009 film *Sherlock Holmes*. The American actor reprised his role as the dapper sleuth in Ritchie's 2011 sequel: *Sherlock Holmes: A Game of Shadows*. Starred alongside Jude Law, who played Watson in both films.

Geoffrey Edwards – Starred in the 1953 revival of a revised version of *The Return of Sherlock Holmes* at the New Theatre, Bromley, from 20 January.

Walter Edwards – Starred in a well-received American stage version of *The Sign of Four*, first produced at the West End Theater, New York, on 9 November 1903.

Stig Ericsson – Played Holmes in two episodes of Swedish Channel 1's series *Master Detectives and Other Smart People* (broadcast 26 and 28 September 1967).

Rupert Everett – British actor with matinee idol looks who starred in *Sherlock Holmes and the Case of the Silk Stocking* by Alan Cubitt, a Tiger Aspect production for the BBC that aired on 26 December 2004. A sequel to the 2002 version of *The Hound of the Baskervilles*, Ian Hart reprised his role as Watson.

Hugo Flink – German actor who appeared in a series of films made by Kowo-Film AG, Germany. Due to the First World War, their release was delayed by several years. The somewhat sensational titles were *The Earthquake Motor*, *The Casket*, *The Snake Ring* (all 1917) and *The Indian Spider* (1918).

Francis Ford – American character actor, brother of Westerns director John Ford, who appeared only once as Holmes in a 1914 adaptation of *A Study in Scarlet* by Gold Seal (Universal), scripted by his wife Grace Cunard.

Barry Foster – Tousle-haired lead actor in minor roles, he took on the mantle of Holmes for a 13-part BBC Birmingham series of adaptations, aired from 4 June to 27 August 1978.

Matt Frewer – Lanky American actor, famous for playing Max Headroom in the early 1980s, who featured in four child-friendly stories for Canadian film company Muse Entertainment. Three canonical adaptations – *The Hound of the Baskervilles* (2000), *The Royal Scandal* (2001, based on *A Scandal in Bohemia*) and *The Sign of Four* (2001) – were followed by a new one by Rodney Gibbons, *The Case of the Whitechapel Vampire* (2002). All four co-starred Kenneth Welsh as Watson.

Martin Fric – Czech actor who appeared in *Lelicek in the Service of Sherlock Homes* (1932), made by Elektafilm AS, Czechoslovakia.

Richard Franklin – Appeared in *Sherlock Holmes of Baker Street* (an amalgam of *A Case of Identity*, *The Mazarin Stone* and *The Dying Detective*), first performed at the Ipswich Drama Centre on 6 November 1974.

John Gielgud – Noted Shakespearean actor who teamed up with Ralph Richardson as Watson in *The Adventures of Sherlock Holmes* (1954), a radio series by Harry Alan Towers for the BBC Light Programme. The 12 adaptations ran from 5 October to 21 December 1954 (with **Orson Welles** as Moriarty in *The Final Problem*).

Robert Gilbert – Appeared in the 1922 UK provincial tour of Doyle's play *The Speckled Band*.

William Gillette – In 1898, Doyle produced a play called *Sherlock Holmes* and sent it to actor-manager Herbert Beerbohm

Tree but, when Tree demanded changes, Doyle lost interest in it. Doyle's literary agent then sent it to American theatrical manager Charles Frohman who passed it to popular stage actor William Gillette. Gillette rewrote Doyle's play (basing it mainly on *A Scandal in Bohemia* and *The Final Problem*), but the manuscript was destroyed in a San Francisco hotel fire. Gillette wrote out the whole play again, and in May 1899 he visited England to seek Doyle's approval. After touring in Buffalo, Syracuse and Rochester, it received its Broadway premiere at the Garrick Theater, New York, on 6 November 1899. Its UK premiere was on 2 September 1901 at the Shakespeare Theatre, Liverpool.

The play ran for 236 performances in New York, after which Gillette toured America until summer 1901. When the London run finished in April 1902 (after 216 performances), four companies toured the country with various Sherlock Holmes, including Gillette himself for eight weeks after the London run. In America, the play was remounted nine times, only once without Gillette, culminating in his farewell tour in 1932. In the UK, it received its third outing in 1974 (see **John Wood**). In 1905, Charles Chaplin played the role of page-boy Billy at the Duke of York's Theatre.

In all, Gillette played the role over 1,200 times and was for many the definitive Holmes. His play encouraged many imitators, including one written by himself called *The Painful Predicament of Sherlock Holmes*, in which a lady client doesn't allow the detective to get a word in edgeways. Its first UK performance was at the Duke of York's Theatre, London, on 3 October 1905.

After such a successful theatrical career, it comes as a surprise to discover that he only made one film, entitled simply *Sherlock Holmes* (1916). As the title suggests, it was a version of his own stage play, slightly opened out by scriptwriter HS Sheldon and filmed in Chicago by the Essanay company. He twice appeared on radio: *The Speckled Band* was the first in a 35-episode series called *The Adventures of Sherlock Holmes* on WEAF-NBC, USA, in 1930 (**Richard Gordon** continued in the role) and an adaptation of his stage play for WABC followed on 18 November 1935.

Julian Glover – Respected stage and film actor who featured in *Sherlock's Last Case* by Matthew Lang (a pseudonym for Charles Marowitz) performed at the Open Space Theatre, London, from 24 July 1974.

R Goodyer-Kettley – Appeared in the UK provincial tour of Doyle's play *The Speckled Band* from December 1914.

Richard Gordon – Featured in three American radio series of *The Adventures of Sherlock Holmes* for WEAF-NBC and WJZ-NBC from 20 October 1930 to 31 May 1933 (the first episode starring **William Gillette**). Gordon gave way to **Louis Hector** for the fourth series, but returned for another one, titled simply *Sherlock Holmes*, from 1 February to 24 December 1936, transmitted on WOR-MBS and WEAF-NBC.

Henri Gouget – Starred in the 1911 two–reel French film *The Adventures of Sherlock Holmes*, directed and written by Victorin Jasset.

A Corney Grain – Appeared in the UK provincial tour of Doyle's play *The Speckled Band* from July 1910.

Stewart Granger – Handsome English swashbuckler of the 1940s and 1950s who appeared in Universal's cheap TV remake of *The Hound of the Baskervilles* in 1972.

Richard E Grant – Tall eccentric actor who appeared as Holmes in *The Other Side*, a TV play by David Ashton broadcast on BBC2 on 29 August 1992.

Mark Greenstreet – Played the central role in *Sherlock Holmes and the Crucifer of Blood*, a UK production of the Mobil Touring Theatre. It toured extensively from February to May 1993.

Bruno Güttner – Hitler's favourite Sherlock Holmes, Güttner featured in *The Hound of the Baskervilles* (1937), produced by German film company Ondra-Lamac-Film GmbH, one of three Holmes films made that year. The detective was brought up to date with polo-neck jersey and leather overcoat.

Larry Hagman – Texan actor most famous for JR Ewing in *Dallas* who played Los Angeles cop Sherman Holmes who thinks he's really Sherlock in *The Return of the World's Greatest Detective* (Universal TV, 1976), a pilot for a never-produced series which owed a lot to *They Might Be Giants* (see **George C Scott**).

Robert Hardy – Extrovert English actor who appeared in eight LP adaptations by Michael and Mollie Hardwick for Discourses Ltd in 1970.

Cedric Hardwicke – British stage actor who made a great many films for Hollywood, appeared in the 1945 BBC Home Service production of *The Adventure of the Speckled Band*, adapted by John Dickson Carr. He was the father of Edward Hardwicke, who later played Watson in the Granada TV series opposite **Jeremy Brett**.

Gerald Harper – Prolific English character actor who took over from **Keith Michell** in the UK production of *The Crucifer of Blood* at the Theatre Royal, Haymarket, from 10 September 1979.

Denys Hawthorne – Starred in *The Man Who Was Sherlock Holmes* by Michael Hardwick (BBC Radio 4, 22 June 1980).

Roger Heathcott – Appeared in the Colchester Repertory

Theatre production of *Sherlock Holmes and the Speckled Band* in December 1968.

Louis Hector – American actor who starred in the fourth radio series of *The Adventures of Sherlock Holmes* broadcast on WJZ-NBC, USA, from 11 November 1934 to 26 May 1935. He went on to play the first television Sherlock Holmes in *The Three Garridebs*, shown live on NBC in 1937.

OP Heggie – Star of the London revival of Doyle's play *The Speckled Band* at the Strand Theatre in February 1911. He later toured with it.

Guy Henry – 22-year-old RADA student who played a teenage Holmes in the eight-part Granada series *Young Sherlock*, subtitled *The Mystery of the Manor House*. It aired from 31 October to 19 December 1982.

Charlton Heston – Hollywood icon who starred in *The Crucifer of Blood* at the Ahmanson Theatre, Los Angeles, with **Jeremy Brett** as Watson. It ran from 5 December 1980 to 17 January 1981. A decade later he reprised the role in a TV movie of the play directed by his son Fraser C Heston. It was shown on TNT (New York) on 4 November 1991.

Anthony Higgins – Played Holmes in the stage play *The White Glove* by Richard Maher and Roger Michell at the Lyric Theatre, Hammersmith, from 21 April to 21 May 1983; and again in the 1993 TV movie *1994 Baker Street: Sherlock Holmes Returns*.

Carleton Hobbs – English character actor who was *the* voice of Sherlock Holmes on BBC radio from 1944 to 1969. He did three BBC Home Service series of *Sherlock Holmes Stories* for Children's Hour (1952–7), and then seven *Sherlock Holmes* series for the Light Programme (1959–69), of which series five was called *Sherlock Holmes Returns*, and six was *Sherlock Holmes Again*. He also appeared in over a dozen one-off adaptations on the Home Service and Light Programme, including the Gillette play in 1953. His Watson was almost invariably Norman Shelley.

Harold Holland – Appeared on Leo Trood's UK tour of **William Gillette**'s play *Sherlock Holmes* from February 1919.

Patrick Horgan – Appeared in the American tour of the 1974 *Sherlock Holmes* stage revival. (See **John Wood**.)

Ronald Howard – Son of Leslie Howard, this British actor appeared in 39 short films made for television by Guild Films of France in 1954, under the umbrella title *Sherlock Holmes*. Sheldon Reynolds directed, and the stories (most of them original) were at best mediocre. Filmed mainly in Paris with an English and French cast, the series has never been shown on British television. Watson actor **Howard Marion-Crawford** had previously played Holmes on radio in 1948.

Noel Howlett – Appeared in **William Gillette**'s play *Sherlock Holmes* at the Repertory Theatre, Northampton, in April 1930.

Richard Hurndall – British character actor who appeared in a five-part radio adaptation of *The Sign of Four* for the BBC Light Programme from 16 May to 13 June 1959.

Marcel Imhoff – Actor in six-part Swiss radio series *Sherlock Holmes* for Radio Suisse Romande, beginning May 1967.

Bauman Karoly – Hungarian actor who appeared in *Sherlock Hochmes*, a 1908 film notable for its synchronised musical accompaniment played on gramophone records.

Edmund Kennedy – Toured in the UK production of *The Holmeses of Baker Street* from July to December 1933. (See **Felix Aylmer**.)

Otto Lagoni – Danish star of the oddly titled 1910 Nordisk picture *Sherlock Holmes in The Claws of the Confidence Men* or *The Stolen Wallet* (UK: *The Confidence Trick*).

Dinsdale Landen – Having played Watson opposite **Robert Powell**, Landen took the main role in the BBC Radio 4 adaptation of *Sherlock's Last Case* on 6 May 1989 (see **Frank Langella**).

Frank Langella – American actor who appeared in an HBO TV movie version of the *Sherlock Holmes* 1974 stage revival. Taped at the Williamstown Theatre Festival, Massachusetts, it was first shown in America on 15 November 1981. In 1987 he starred in Charles Marowitz's revised version of *Sherlock's Last Case* at the Eisenhower Theater, Washington DC (1 July to 1 August) and at the Nederlander Theatre, New York (20 August to 6 December). (See **Dinsdale Landen**.)

Viggo Larsen – Short, stocky Danish actor who directed, wrote and starred in a series of Holmes films made by the Nordisk Films Kompagni of Copenhagen at the beginning of the twentieth century. *Sherlock Holmes Risks His Life* (UK: *Sherlock Holmes*) kicked off the series in 1908. This was swiftly followed the same year by *Sherlock Holmes II* (UK: *Raffles Escapes from Prison*) and *Sherlock Holmes III* (UK: *Sherlock Holmes in the Gas Cellar* or *The Theft of the State Document*). The next year came *The Singer's Diamonds* (UK: *The Theft of the Diamonds*), *Cab No.519* and *The Grey Lady*. This latter production followed the plot of *The Hound of the Baskervilles* quite closely, although it replaced the Hound with the Grey Lady of the title. A series of five short films was released in 1910 under the banner title *Arsène Lupin Against Sherlock Holmes*, all directed by and starring Larsen, with Paul Otto as Lupin. (Lupin's creator Maurice Leblanc had to publish his book version as the thinly-disguised *Arsène Lupin Against Herlock Sholmes*, but the filmmakers got away with the detective's real name.) Production was shared between Vitascope GmbH in Germany and Nordisk Films in Denmark. Two further films followed in

1912, both made by Vitascope: *The End of Arsène Lupin* and *Sherlock Holmes Against Professor Moriarty* (aka *The Heir of Bloomrod*). Messter-Film's *Rotterdam-Amsterdam* in 1918 proved to be his swansong.

Peter Lawford – Rat Pack actor who appeared as Holmes in a *Fantasy Island* segment entitled *Save Sherlock Holmes*, first transmitted in America on 6 February 1982. Donald O'Connor, best remembered as Cosmo Brown in *Singin' in the Rain* (1952), played his Watson.

John Lawson – Music-hall performer who wrote and starred in *An Adventure in the Life of Sherlock Holmes*, first performed at the Paragon Music Hall, Mile End Road, London, on 6 January 1902; later rewritten with **W R Perceval** as Holmes.

Christopher Lee – British horror actor, the most prolific of his generation, who played a deliberately unlikeable Holmes in the poor 1962 West German production, *Sherlock Holmes and the Deadly Necklace* (1962). He and Thorley Walters (Watson) spoke English while the rest of the German cast acted in their native tongue, but when the film was later released their voices were dubbed by unknown American actors. The director was Terence Fisher, responsible for Hammer's *The Hound of the Baskervilles* three years earlier. More recently, Lee has resumed the mantle of the Great Detective in two TV movies, *Sherlock Holmes and the Leading Lady* (1990) and *Sherlock Holmes: The Incident at Victoria Falls* (1991), the latter filmed in South Africa. Patrick Macnee played Watson, as he had done before with **Roger Moore** in *Sherlock Holmes in New York*.

Charles H Lester – Toured the UK provinces with *The Bank of England* from 1900 (see **John F Preston**).

H Lawrence Leyton – Appeared on the UK tour of **William Gillette**'s play *Sherlock Holmes* from August 1905.

Rupert Lister – Featured in the 1923 UK provincial tour of

Doyle's play *The Speckled Band*.

Vasily Livanov – Muscovite actor (son of Boris Livanov, once described as the Russian Olivier) who starred in several well-made adaptations for Russian television made by Lenfilms. Titles include: *Acquaintance* (1979), *Sherlock Holmes and Doctor Watson* (1979), *The Bloody Signature* (1979), *The Adventures of Sherlock Holmes and Doctor Watson* (1980), *The Hound of the Baskervilles* (1981), *The Treasures of Agra* (1983) and *The Twentieth Century Begins* (1986).

Roger Llewellyn – Starred in Chris Martin's version of *The Hound of the Baskervilles* at the New Vic, Newcastle-under-Lyme, in the summer of 1997; and then in David Stuart Davies' one-man play *Sherlock Holmes – The Last Act!*, first performed at the Salisbury Playhouse on 18 May 1999. He has since toured with this play in Britain, Canada, America and elsewhere.

John Longden – British leading man of the 1930s. In 1951, he starred in a film version of *The Man with the Twisted Lip*, the first in a proposed series for television by the British company Vandyke Pictures. The series never got made, so the film languished in the cinemas as a supporting feature.

Radovan Lukavsky – Prague-born actor who featured in *The Longing of Sherlock Holmes* (Czechoslovak Film, 1971), concerning his descent into crime!

Kenneth Macmillan – English dancer who played the title role as well as 'The Infamous Professor' in Margaret Dale and Richard Arnell's ballet *The Great Detective*, first performed at Sadler's Wells, London, on 21 January 1953.

Patrick Macnee – After playing Watson to **Roger Moore** and **Christopher Lee**, this former *Avengers* star took on the mantle of Holmes in the Canadian TV movie version of Craig Bowlsby's play *The Hound of London*, first transmitted in 1993.

Hugh Manning – Played Holmes in selected scenes from Gillette's stage play as part of the first BBC stereo transmission on 15 November 1958. To achieve the required effect, the scenes were shown on BBC TV with half the sound coming from the TV speaker and half from a strategically placed radio speaker.

Howard Marion-Crawford – Sporty British actor (sometimes billed without the hyphen) who starred in a BBC Home Service adaptation of *The Adventure of the Speckled Band* (with an introduction by Adrian Conan Doyle) on 26 December 1948. He later played Watson in the French TV series opposite **Ronald Howard**.

Roy Marsden – Played Holmes in dramatisations by Grant Eustace released on audio cassette in October 1990.

Raymond Massey – Canadian-born actor who played saturnine villains. His screen debut was in British & Dominion's *The Speckled Band* (1931) in which he made a reasonable stab at Holmes opposite scenery-chewing Lyn Harding as Moriarty. The screenplay by WP Lipscombe was adapted from Doyle's stage play.

Francis Matthews – Played Holmes in Brian Clemens' stage play *Holmes and the Ripper* at the Theatre Royal, Brighton, from 25 July 1988, and then on a national tour.

Clive Merrison – Alongside Michael Williams as Watson, Merrison appeared in adaptations of every Sherlock Holmes story for BBC Radio 4. The series ran from 5 November 1989 to 29 March 1995, with *The Hound of the Baskervilles* (first made with **Roger Rees** as a pilot) following three years later, from 28 June to 5 July 1998. Later, ten new adventures by Bert Coules, entitled *The Further Adventures of Sherlock Holmes*, ran from 30 January 2002 to 15 June 2004, with Andrew Sachs as Watson.

Keith Michell – Popular classical actor who starred in *The Crucible of Blood* when it received its UK premiere at the Theatre Royal, Haymarket, on 15 March 1979. **Paxton Whitehead** was the original Broadway Holmes.

Charles Millward – American star of Doyle's play *The Speckled Band*, which received its US premiere on 21 November 1910 at the Garrick Theater, New York (see **HA Saintsbury**).

John Moffatt – Appeared in the BBC Radio 4 play *Sherlock Holmes vs. Dracula*, written, produced and directed by Glyn Dearman. It was broadcast in the UK on 19 December 1981. He later played Watson opposite **Dinsdale Landen** and **Roy Marsden**.

Ron Moody – British character actor in humorous roles, and the star of *Sherlock Holmes – The Musical* (music, lyrics and book by Leslie Bricusse) which opened at the Northcott Theatre, Exeter on 18 October 1988.

Alan Moore – Star of the 1970 revival of Doyle's play *The Speckled Band*, performed from 22 September to 10 October at the Library Theatre, Manchester.

Eugene Moore – Appeared in the American production of **John F Preston**'s *The Bank of England* at the Grand Theatre, New York, in February 1904.

Roger Moore – Square-jawed British James Bond actor who was rather too suave for the TV movie *Sherlock Holmes in New York*, made by 20th Century Fox, and shown in America on 18 October 1976 (opposite Patrick Macnee as Watson). A proposed series never materialised.

Alan Napier – Born in Birmingham, this tall, dapper British character is best known for playing Alfred the butler in the 1960s TV series *Batman*. A regular guest star on American television, in 1949 he played Holmes in *The Adventure of the Speckled*

Band, an episode of the television anthology series *Your Show Time* which featured dramatised short stories by famous authors such as Guy de Maupassant and Robert Louis Stevenson. The 25-minute Marshall-Grant-Realm Television production was directed by Sobey Martin.

Harold V Neilson – Appeared in his own touring company's 1917 UK production of Doyle's play *The Speckled Band*.

Dennis Neilson-Terry – English actor who appeared in Doyle's second play, *The Crown Diamond*, a one-act melodrama first performed at the London Coliseum on 16 May 1921 for a week (followed by another week in August).

Alwin Neuss – First seen as Holmes in the 1910 Nordisk Films Kompagni production of *The One Million Bond* (UK: *The Stolen Legacy* or *Sherlock Holmes's Masterpiece*). In 1914 he began a series of German adaptations for Vitascope GmbH. *The Hound of the Baskervilles* (1914) was a fairly prestigious production, with sets designed by the Expressionist Hermann Warm who four years later worked on *The Cabinet of Dr Caligari*. It was followed by three far-fetched sequels: *The Isolated House* (1914), *The Uncanny Room* (1915) – up against a rival production (see **Eugen Burg**) – and *How the Hound of the Baskervilles Arose* (1915). A stand-alone story, *A Scream in the Night*, followed later that year. (Two further *Hound of the Baskervilles* sequels were released c.1920 – *Dr Macdonald's Sanatorium* and *The House Without Windows* – but casting details are scarce.)

John Neville – Shakespearean actor who starred in *A Study in Terror* (1965), an impressive British film produced by Compton-Tekli in conjunction with Sir Nigel Films, a company formed by the Sir Arthur Conan Doyle Estate to film the late author's stories. The plot has Holmes fighting Jack the Ripper, and the film remains one of the best big-screen adaptations, due mainly to James Hill's convincing direction.

Neville also appeared in the American production of the 1974 *Sherlock Holmes* revival (see **John Wood**).

Leonard Nimoy – *Star Trek*'s Mr Spock who appeared on the US tour of the 1974 *Sherlock Holmes* revival. (See **John Wood**.) A year later, he made a rightfully obscure 1975 Kentucky Educational TV programme called *The Interior Motive*, in which Holmes explained the formation of the earth!

Eille Norwood – London-based film company Stoll Picture Productions snapped up this 59-year-old British stage actor (real name Anthony Brett) to play a very authentic-looking Holmes in 1920. The first series of fifteen 30-minute shorts were known collectively as *The Adventures of Sherlock Holmes*, released in April 1921 to be used as supporting features. A feature-length *Hound of the Baskervilles* followed in August of that year. All were directed by Maurice Elvey, and co-starred Hubert Willis as Watson. Although they were updated to the 1920s, Doyle praised the films as being 'quite wonderful'.

Another 15 films followed in 1922, collectively *The Further Adventures of Sherlock Holmes*. The director was George Ridgewell. The next year saw the third and final Stoll series, *The Last Adventures of Sherlock Holmes*, again directed by Ridgewell. *The Sign of Four* was the last film to star Norwood as Holmes. Released in 1923, it was scripted and directed by Maurice Elvey. The same year Norwood produced and starred in the stage play *The Return of Sherlock Holmes* (written by his nephew JE Harold-Terry) which received its London premiere at the Princes Theatre, Shaftesbury Avenue, on 9 October.

Andrew Osborn – Played the first TV Sherlock Holmes in the UK, in *The Mazarin Stone* (BBC, 29 July 1951), a pilot for a series starring **Alan Wheatley**. He went on to produce BBC's *Maigret*.

Henry Oscar – Appeared in the 1922 UK provincial tour of

Doyle's play *The Speckled Band*.

Peter O'Toole – The voice of Holmes in American cartoon adaptations of Conan Doyle's four novels in 1983, one retitled *The Baskerville Curse*.

Reginald Owen – After playing Watson to **Clive Brook**'s Holmes, Owen himself starred as the Great Detective in *A Study in Scarlet* (1933) for World Wide, USA, a film he co-wrote with Robert Florey.

Geoffrey Palmer – Grizzled British actor who starred in *The Mask of Moriarty* at the Haymarket Theatre, Leicester. The performance ran from 11 June to 11 July 1987.

Michael Pennington – Starred in the US TV movie *The Return of Sherlock Holmes*, in which the Great Detective is discovered in suspended animation by Watson's great-grand-daughter Jane. It aired in America on 10 January 1987.

WR Perceval – Star of the rewritten play *An Adventure in the Life of Sherlock Holmes*, first performed at the Theatre Royal, Garston, Liverpool, on 8 May 1902 (see **John Lawson**).

Ronald Pickup – Silky-voiced British actor who appeared in BBC Radio 3 play *The Singular Case of Sherlock H and Sigmund F* by Cecil Jenkins. It was transmitted on 6 February 1990.

Tim Pigott-Smith – Starred in *The Valley of Fear*, adapted by Roy Apps and broadcast on BBC Radio 4 on 24 May 1986.

Christopher Plummer – Canadian actor, cousin of Nigel Bruce, who appeared as Holmes in the 1977 HTV adaptation of *Silver Blaze*. A year later he was in *Murder by Decree*, a Saucy Jack/Decree film directed by Bob Clark that had Holmes investigating the Ripper murders (as in *A Study in Terror*).

Robert Powell – Enigmatic British leading man who appeared in a BBC radio version of *A Study in Scarlet* trans-mitted on Christmas Day 1974. In 1993 he toured with *Sherlock Holmes – The Musical* (see **Ron Moody**).

Tim Preece – Tall, thin supporting actor who starred in the Perth Repertory Theatre's production of *The Hound of the Baskervilles* in April 1971.

John F Preston – Stage name for dramatist Max Goldberg who appeared in his own play *The Bank of England* at the Shakespeare Theatre, Clapham, from November 1900. Provincial tours followed.

Ian Price – Featured in the Bristol Old Vic Theatre Company's production of *The Crucifer of Blood* at the Theatre Royal, Bristol, from 23 November to 17 December 1983.

Holgar Rasmussen – Starred in the 1911 film *The Black Hand* (aka *Murder in Baker Street*) made by the Nordisk Films Kompagni. In the UK it was probably called *The Conspirators*.

Basil Rathbone – Born in South Africa but raised in England, this quintessentially British actor with clipped diction and an angular jaw had spent most of his career playing villains before being cast as Sherlock Holmes (allegedly over a Hollywood dinner party) by 20th Century Fox supremo Darryl F Zanuck. His first film, yet another adaptation of *The Hound of the Baskervilles*, was made in 1939 and was the first to use the original Victorian setting. In it Rathbone was joined by the bumbling but immensely likeable Nigel Bruce as Watson.

The Adventures of Sherlock Holmes (UK: *Sherlock Holmes*) came out later that year, again true to period, and conjuring up a convincing evocation of gaslit, foggy London. Inexplicably, Fox then dropped the pair and they moved to Universal where they starred in a dozen updated and generally less well-made features. 1942: *Sherlock Holmes and the Voice of Terror* (working title: *Sherlock Holmes Saves London*), *Sherlock Holmes and the Secret Weapon*, *Sherlock Holmes in Washington*. 1943: *Sherlock Holmes Faces Death*. 1944: *Sherlock Holmes and the Spider Woman*, *The Scarlet Claw*, *The Pearl of Death*. 1945: *The House of Fear*, *The*

Woman in Green, *Pursuit to Algiers*. 1946: *Terror By Night*, *Dressed To Kill* (UK: *Sherlock Holmes and the Secret Code*). Some claimed they were based on Doyle's original stories, but in most cases the resemblance was only passing. For a while Rathbone had to contend with the silliest haircut in cinema history, and although there were some triumphs (notably *The Scarlet Claw* and *Dressed to Kill*), the fast production schedule and low budgets meant that most were not as good as they could have been. But Rathbone and Bruce proved to be the most popular Holmes and Watson yet and, for decades, they were the archetypal Baker Street sleuths.

Alongside the films, Rathbone and Bruce appeared in 213 half-hour American radio broadcasts, covering all the original stories plus ones only alluded to in the canon (such as the giant rat of Sumatra), together with plenty of brand new cases. The series ran from October 1939 to May 1946. In 1953, Rathbone returned to the role that had made him famous. *The Black Baronet* was shown in May (as part of the CBS TV series *Suspense*, adapted from a story by Adrian Conan Doyle and John Dickson Carr) while in October he appeared on stage in *Sherlock Holmes*, written by his wife Ouida. It ran for three weeks in Boston, but flopped in New York where it was taken off after only three days.

Roy Redgrave – Wrote and starred in *The Great Detective*, first performed at Sadler's Wells on 13 January 1902.

Roger Rees – Urbane leading man who starred in a BBC radio adaptation of *The Hound of the Baskervilles* in May 1988. He was replaced by **Clive Merrison** for a mammoth run of the entire series.

Robert Rendel – British actor who made a career out of playing toffs in the 1930s, appeared in Gainsborough Picture's *The Hound of the Baskervilles* in 1932, with additional dialogue by mystery writer Edgar Wallace.

Henry Renouf – Appeared on the UK tour of **William Gillette**'s play *Sherlock Holmes* from August 1905.

Ian Richardson – Dour Scottish actor whose career playing figures of authority set him up perfectly to play Holmes in TV adaptations of *The Sign of Four* and *The Hound of the Baskervilles*, both made in England in 1983 by Sy Weintraub's Mapleton Films company. Richardson appeared as Dr Joseph Bell, the inspiration for Sherlock Holmes, in the series *Murder Rooms* (2000). Bell plays Holmes to Conan Doyle's Dr Watson, and their cases involve other literary creations. For example, Professor Challenger is in an episode scripted by Stephen Gallagher.

Miles Richardson – Son of the above; played Holmes in *Sherlock Holmes: The Adventure at Sir Arthur Sullivan's* by Tim Heath, first performed at the Komedia Theatre, Brighton, on 11 September 1996. A British tour followed.

Kenneth Rivington – English stage actor who appeared in the Midland Company's touring production of *Sherlock Holmes* from January 1904 to May 1905 (see **William Gillette**). When not playing Holmes, he played Watson – the first actor to play both parts (others are **Reginald Owen, Carleton Hobbs, Howard Marion-Crawford, Jeremy Brett** and **Patrick Macnee**).

Sam Robinson – The only black actor to play Sherlock Holmes in any medium, Robinson starred in the Ebony Pictures production of *Black Sherlock Holmes* (1918), directed by RW Phillips.

Nicholas Rowe – British actor who starred in Barry Levinson's 1986 film *Young Sherlock Holmes* (UK: *Sherlock Holmes and the Pyramid of Fear*). Although well-made, it was a box-office disappointment.

Richard Roxburgh – Australian actor who starred in a no-holds-barred adaptation of *The Hound of the Baskervilles* by Tiger Aspect Productions for the BBC, transmitted on 26 December 2002. Ian Hart played Watson.

Julian Royce – English stage actor who appeared in the South Company's touring production of *Sherlock Holmes* from March 1902 to May 1904 (see **William Gillette**). He later toured with Doyle's *The Speckled Band* from July 1910 (see **HA Saintsbury**).

HA Saintsbury – Dignified actor who took part in the UK tour of **William Gillette**'s *Sherlock Holmes* play from March 1902 to June 1905, and went on to star in Doyle's own play *The Speckled Band*, first performed at the Adelphi Theatre, London, on 4 June 1910 (followed by numerous tours). He appeared on film in GB Samuelson's 1916 production of *The Valley of Fear*, later reviving the Gillette role for a 1926 theatre run.

Fred Sargent – Appeared on the UK tour of **William Gillette**'s play *Sherlock Holmes* from 26 December 1901.

Cyril Scott – Cast as Holmes in the American run of *The Holmeses of Baker Street* at the Masque Theater, New York, from 9 December 1936. (See **Felix Aylmer**.)

George C Scott – Gruff American actor. He appeared in Universal Pictures' *They Might Be Giants* (1971), a film adaptation of James Goldman's play about a lawyer called Justin Playfair who assumes the identity of Sherlock Holmes. **Harry H Corbett** was the unlikely choice for the stage version ten years earlier.

TA Shannon – Appeared on the UK tour of *Sherlock Holmes* from 26 December 1901 (see **William Gillette**).

Sebastian Shaw – Starred in *The Adventure of the Speckled Band*, dramatised by John Dickson Carr for the BBC radio's

Overseas Service in September 1956.

Tod Slaughter – Barnstorming performer who starred in his own touring company's production of *The Return of Sherlock Holmes* (see **Eille Norwood**) in October and November 1928.

Hermann Speelmans – German-born actor who played a chubby-faced criminal called Jimmy Ward (Sherlock Holmes in disguise) in *Sherlock Holmes: The Grey Lady* (1937, Neue Film KG).

Brent Spiner – Impersonated Holmes for an episode of *Star Trek: The Next Generation* called *Elementary, Dear Data* (first transmitted in America on 12 May 1988).

John Stanley – Took over for two further American radio series of *Sherlock Holmes* after **Tom Conway** left. A total of 76 stories were transmitted on WOR-MBS from 28 September 1947 to 6 June 1949.

Herbert Stanton – Starred in the UK provincial tour of Doyle's play *The Speckled Band* from December 1914.

H Hamilton Stewart – Appeared in his own touring company's production of **William Gillette**'s play *Sherlock Holmes* from August 1906 to December 1917 in the UK.

Robert Stephens – English classical actor and assistant director of the National Theatre chosen by Billy Wilder to star in *The Private Life of Sherlock Holmes* (United Artists/Phalanx/Mirisch/Sir Nigel Films) in 1970. Holmes was portrayed as a real person rather than the caricature he had become, but the intense emotional drain nearly killed Stephens. **Christopher Lee** played Mycroft Holmes. The $10m three-hour film was pruned back to two prior to its release, but proved a box-office disappointment despite its excellent production values. He also appeared in the American production of the 1974 *Sherlock Holmes* revival. (See **John**

Wood.)

Edward Stirling – Played Holmes in the French production of Doyle's *The Speckled Band*, performed in the summer of 1925 at the Théâtre Albert, Paris.

Mark Tandy – English stage and television actor who appeared in Chris Martin's adaptation of *A Study in Scarlet* (directed by Michael Crompton) which was performed at the Greenwich Theatre, London, from 30 November 1989 to 20 January 1990.

Leonard Tremayne – Appeared in Leo Trood's UK tour of **William Gillette**'s play *Sherlock Holmes* from February 1919.

Georges Tréville – French actor who appeared in an otherwise all-British cast when the French film company Eclair produced eight 15-minute films based on Doyle's original stories in 1912. Filmed at the Kursaal, Bexhill-on-Sea, they were *The Speckled Band*, *The Reigate Squires*, *The Beryl Coronet*, *The Adventure of the Copper Beeches*, *A Mystery of Boscombe Vale*, *The Stolen Papers* (from the story *The Naval Treaty*), *Silver Blaze* and *The Musgrave Ritual*. Directed by Tréville, they stuck quite rigidly to Doyle's original narratives (with a few notable exceptions, such as having no Watson in the first film).

Leo Trood – Appeared in his own company's UK tour of **William Gillette**'s play *Sherlock Holmes* from February 1919.

E Vassal Vaughan – Appeared in the UK provincial tour of Doyle's play *The Speckled Band* from September 1910.

Kevin Vaughn – American actor who starred in the musical *Holmes!* (book and lyrics by Brett Nicholson, music by Hans Vollrath). It premiered at the Disney Institute, Florida, on 23 September 1997 and has had several workshop performances since, including a benefit concert for the Civic Theatres of Central Florida.

Robert Warwick – Appeared in the ninth American production of the 1899 *Sherlock Holmes* stage play at the Cosmopolitan Theater, New York, premiering on 20 February 1928. (See **William Gillette**.)

Fritz Weaver – American stage actor who starred in the successful 1965 musical *Baker Street* (book by Jerome Coopersmith, music and lyrics by Marian Grudeff and Raymond Jessell, directed by Harold Prince). It premiered on 16 February at the Broadway Theater, New York and ran for 313 performances.

John Webb – In December 1893, the same time that Holmes met his 'death' at the Reichenbach Falls, the five-act play *Sherlock Holmes, Private Detective* received its copyright performance at the Theatre Royal, Hanley, Stoke-on-Trent, with Webb in the main role. As *Sherlock Holmes: A Psychological Drama in Five Acts*, it began touring on 28 May 1894 at the Theatre Royal, Glasgow, and continued until at least April 1902. Charles Rogers was the dramatist, and it was quite strong stuff for its time. **Henry S Dacre** took over at some point in the run.

Orson Welles – Charismatic character actor who directed and starred in a radio production of Gillette's stage play *Sherlock Holmes* on 25 September 1938 as part of the *Mercury Theatre On The Air* series for American station WABC-CS. He later played Moriarty on radio opposite **John Gielgud**.

Alan Wheatley – Debonair British actor who first appeared as Holmes in a high-profile six-part series for the BBC (20 October to 1 December 1951), scripted by *Observer* film critic CA Lejeune. He was later called in for a BBC Home Service *Tribute to Sherlock Holmes* on 8 January 1954.

Geoffrey Whitehead – British actor who starred in *Sherlock Holmes and Doctor Watson*, a 1982 Polish series masterminded by Sheldon Reynolds, director of the 1954 French series with

Ronald Howard. Most of the 22 episodes were original stories and, like the 1954 series, it has never been shown in the UK.

Paxton Whitehead – American actor who appeared in *The Crucifer of Blood*, a stage play by Paul Giovanni (based in part on *The Sign of Four*). Appearing briefly in the Studio Arena Theater, Buffalo in January, its Broadway life began on 28 September when it opened at the Helen Hayes Theater, New York. **Charlton Heston** starred in its Los Angeles run, while **Keith Michell** appeared in the UK.

Bransby Williams – Stage actor specialising in character sketches, some from Sherlock Holmes. London Pavilion, from 26 September 1898 (repeated in May 1902).

Nicol Williamson – Bombastic British actor who played Holmes in Nicholas Meyer's film adaptation of his own novel, *The Seven-Per-Cent Solution* (1976), concerning a meeting with Sigmund Freud. (See **Michael Blagdon**.)

Douglas Wilmer – After **Alan Wheatley**'s stab at Holmes in the first BBC television series, Wilmer featured in a pilot for the revamped second series, *The Speckled Band*, on 18 May 1964 (as part of the *Detective* series.) A 12-part series followed in 1965 (20 February to 8 May). Nigel Stock played Watson, continuing for the third series with **Peter Cushing**. He went on to star in Gene Wilder's hit-or-miss comedy film *The Adventures of Sherlock Holmes' Smarter Brother* (TCF/Jouer, 1975), which saw Wilder play Holmes' brother Sigerson ('Sigi').

Mark Wing-Davey – *Hitch-Hiker's Guide to the Galaxy* actor who played Holmes in the BBC radio play *The Mystery of the Reluctant Storyteller* by Derek Wilson. It was transmitted on Radio 4 on 18 January 1986.

Arthur Wontner – Gaunt British actor of the 1930s,

Wontner had already played several detectives (including *Sexton Blake* in 1930), before he was cast as Holmes in five films by London-based company Twickenham Film Studios. Although a little old for the part, his portrayal was entirely convincing and received many glowing accolades – 'accept no substitute', declared one American film critic. *The Sleeping Cardinal* (USA: *Sherlock Holmes' Fatal Hour*) was made in 1931, based on *The Final Problem* and *The Empty House* with elements lifted from the Gillette play. *The Missing Rembrandt* followed in 1932 (based partly on *Charles Augustus Milverton*). The larger Associated Radio Pictures headhunted Wontner for his next picture, *The Sign of Four* (1932). Made at Ealing, this was an Americanised version of the novel with Holmes as a macho action figure. It suffered accordingly.

Twickenham briefly changed its name to Real Art Productions for Wontner's fourth outing, *The Triumph of Sherlock Holmes* (1935), and happily brought Holmes back down to earth again. (The film was made under the title of *The Valley of Fear*, but had its name changed just prior to release.) Moriarty was played by Lyn Harding (Grimesby Rylott in the 1910 stage play *The Speckled Band* – see **HA Saintsbury**). Harding appeared as Moriarty again in the last Wontner film, *Silver Blaze* (USA: *Murder at the Baskervilles*) in 1937. He reprised the role once more for the 1943 BBC radio version of *The Boscombe Valley Mystery*, aged 68, with **Carleton Hobbs** as Watson.

John Wood – Tall English actor, usually cast in snooty roles. He was chosen to star in the Royal Shakespeare Company's 1974 revival of William Gillette's stage play, *Sherlock Holmes*. It premiered on 1 January at the Aldwych Theatre, London, and ran for 106 performances. Wood followed the show to Broadway, later replaced by **Patrick Horgan**, **John**

Neville, **Robert Stephens** and, on tour, **Leonard Nimoy**. The play was recorded for HBO in 1981 with **Frank Langella**.

Edward Woodward – Starred in a 1990 UK television film, *Hands of a Murderer* (aka: *Sherlock Holmes and the Prince of Crime*) made by Yorkshire/Green Pond/Storke Productions.

Ben Wright – Took over from **John Stanley** for the final 39-part American radio series of *The Adventures of Sherlock Holmes* (WJZ-ABC) from 21 September 1949 to 14 June 1950.

Charles York – Appeared in *The Heart of London* stage play at the Theatre Royal, Goole, from 12 March 1906, and then in the UK provincial tour of Doyle's play *The Speckled Band* from December 1914. (It is possible that 'C York' in the 1906 play might be a different actor.)

HA Young – Appeared in the UK provincial tour of Doyle's play *The Speckled Band* from November 1915 to May 1916.

Reference Materials

Books

The Canon

Individual books are available from a variety of publishers including Penguin Popular Classics (£2), Wordsworth Editions (£2), Oxford Classics (£5.99–£6.99) and Penguin Classics (£5.99–£6.99). They are also available in many different audio formats. The myriad collected volumes include *The Original Illustrated Strand Sherlock Holmes* (Wordsworth, PB, £5.99), *The Penguin Complete Sherlock Holmes* (Penguin, HB, £16.99) and, in audio, *The Complete Sherlock Holmes Box Set* (BBC, 64xCDs, £180) featuring Clive Merrison. The stories are available online at the Camden House website (http://camdenhouse.ignisart.com), amongst others.

About Sherlock Holmes

Fido, Martin, *The World of Sherlock Holmes*, London: Carlton Books, 1998

Hall, Trevor H, *Sherlock Holmes and His Creator*, London: Duckworth, 1978

Nown, Graham, *Elementary, My Dear Watson*, London: Ward Lock, 1986

Rennison, Nick, *Sherlock Holmes: The Unauthorized Biography*,

London: Atlantic Books, 2005
Weller, Philip & Roden, Christopher, *The Life and Times of Sherlock Holmes*, New York: Crescent Books, 1993

Selected Fiction of Arthur Conan Doyle
Micah Clarke (1889): Novel of the 1685 Monmouth Rebellion
The White Company (1891): Fourteenth century knight-errantry with Sir Nigel
The Great Shadow (1892): Novel about the Napoleonic era and Waterloo
The Exploits of Brigadier Gerard (1896): Brigadier Gerard
Rodney Stone (1896): Pre-Regency mystery
Uncle Bernac (1897): Napoleonic novel
The Tragedy of The Korosko (1898): Egyptian adventure novel
The Adventures of Gerard (1903): Brigadier Gerard
Sir Nigel (1906): Fourteenth century knight-errantry with Sir Nigel
The Lost World (1912): Professor Challenger
The Poison Belt (1913): Professor Challenger
The Land of Mist (1926): Professor Challenger

About Arthur Conan Doyle
Costello, Peter, *Conan Doyle, Detective*, London: Constable & Robinson, 2006
Lycett, Andrew, *Conan Doyle: The Man Behind Sherlock Holmes*, London: Weidenfeld & Nicolson, 2007
Norman, Andrew, *Arthur Conan Doyle: Beyond Sherlock Holmes,* Stroud: Tempus Publishing, 2007
Stashower, Daniel, *Teller of Tales: The Life of Arthur Conan Doyle*, Harmondsworth: Penguin, 2000

Media

Davies, David Stuart, *Starring Sherlock Holmes*, London: Titan Books, 2007

Earnshaw, Tony, *An Actor and a Rare One: Peter Cushing as Sherlock Holmes*, Lanham, Maryland: Scarecrow Press, 2001

Eyles, Allen, *Sherlock Holmes – A Centenary Celebration*, London: John Murray, 1986

Haining, Peter, *The Television Sherlock Holmes (Revised),* London: Virgin Books, 1991

Pointer, Michael, *The Public Life of Sherlock Holmes*, Newton Abbot: David & Charles, 1975

Pastiches and Parodies

Chapter 3 contains a fuller listing, but here are some good general anthologies:

Ashley, Mike (ed), *The Mammoth Book of New Sherlock Holmes Adventures*, London: Constable & Robinson, 1997

Green, Richard Lancelyn (ed), *The Further Adventures of Sherlock Holmes*, Harmondsworth: Penguin, 1985

Greenberg, Martin H & Waugh, Carol-Lynn Rössel (eds), *The New Adventures of Sherlock Holmes*, New York: Carroll & Graf, 1987

Haining, Peter (ed), *The Final Adventures of Sherlock Holmes*, London: WH Allen, 1981

DVDs

As you can imagine, there is a vast array of Sherlockiana available to buy on DVD. For the best Internet prices, Amazon and Play are usually the ones to go for, although don't forget to check out Julian Knott's excellent Zeta Minor website (www.zetaminor.com) for the best bargains around, as well as news of upcoming releases. High street retailers, such as HMV or WH Smith, can sometimes match the e-suppliers, but not often. New DVD retailers usually fall by the wayside after a year or two, so always keep an eye on closing down sales to get some really decent bargains (remember MVC?).

Internet

Websites

The Brettish Empire (www.brettish.com) An in-depth assessment of Brett's career, with plenty on the Granada TV series. Maintained by Lisa Oldham.

Camden House: The Complete Sherlock Holmes (http://camdenhouse.ignisart.com) All the original stories online, together with a comprehensive collection of illustrations. An excellent resource.

Sherlock Holmes Atlas (http://www.evo.org/sherlock) Out of date, but nonetheless fascinating concordance of locations referenced in the canon.

Sherlock Holmes Concordance (http://mrmoon.com/moonfind/holmes) Forgot which story Simon Bird appeared in? Simple, just type the name and press 'search'. Search individual books or the entire canon.

Sherlock Holmes Museum (www.sherlock-holmes.co.uk) All the information on Baker Street's museum and shop.

Sherlock Holmes International (http://www.evo.org/sherlock/international) Ideal for Sherlockians worldwide, this site contains all the best links including newsgroups, memorabilia and webrings.

Sherlock Holmes Pub (www.sherlockholmespub.com) If

you want to know what Inspector Lestrade's favourite dish is, log onto the website of this famous Northumberland Avenue hostelry.

Sherlock Holmes Shoppe (www.sherlock-holmes.com) Cincinnati-based retailer that offers a wide range of Holmesiana including calendars, greetings cards and pastiches.

Sherlock Holmes Society of London (www.sherlock-holmes.org.uk) The website of one of the world's foremost societies dedicated to studying and furthering interest in the famous consulting detective. Here you'll find their monthly publication *The District Messenger* (edited by Roger Johnson), always full of the latest news.

Sherlockian.Net (www.sherlockian.net/index.html) An excellent site run by Chris Redmond offering many useful web resources and an especially good section on Holmes actors.

Sherlocktron (http://sherlocktron.hostoi.com/about.the.ads.listing.pdf) An excellent Internet information centre on all things Holmes.

Universal Sherlock Holmes (http://special.lib.umn.edu/rare/ush/ush.html) An invaluable online bibliography by Ronald De Waal that documents the appearances of Sherlock Holmes in every medium.

WelcomeHolmes (http://groups.yahoo.com/group/welcomeholmes) The most active Sherlock Holmes discussion group on the net.

Yoxley Old Place (http://fanlore.org/wiki/Yoxley_Old_Place_-_Sherlock_Holmes_on_the_Web) Subtitled 'Sherlock Holmes on the Web,' this is a nicely thought-out cornucopia of information, links and news.

Newsgroup
alt.fan.holmes The place to go for discussions on absolutely

anything Holmesian.

Contact the author: If you would like to correspond with Mark Campbell, and give him some feedback on this Pocket Essential, please send an email to mark.campbell10@virgin.net.

Index

OTHER TITLES IN THIS SERIES

Or browse all our titles at www.pocketessentials.com

Available from all good bookshops or send a cheque to:

Pocket Essentials (Dept SS),
P.O. Box 394, Harpenden, Herts, AL5 1XJ.

Please make cheques payable to
'Oldcastle Books', add 50p for postage and packing
for each book in the UK and £1 elsewhere.

Customers worldwide can order online at
www.pocketessentials.com